David Thomson

INGRID BERGMAN

David Thomson is, among many other things, the author of *The New Biographical Dictionary of Film*, now in its fourth edition. His recent books include a biography of Nicole Kidman, completing and editing *Fan Tan* (a novel started by Marlon Brando and Donald Cammell), and *The Whole Equation: A History of Hollywood*. His latest work is the acclaimed *Have You Seen . . . ? A Personal Introduction to 1,000 Films*. Born in London, he now lives in San Francisco.

Books in the GREAT STARS Series
by David Thomson

Ingrid Bergman
Humphrey Bogart
Gary Cooper
Bette Davis

INGRID BERGMAN

INGRID BERGMAN

David Thomson

PHOTO RESEARCH BY LUCY GRAY

ff Faber and Faber, Inc.

An affiliate of Farrar, Straus and Giroux

New York

GREAT STARS

For Isaac

Faber and Faber, Inc.
An affiliate of Farrar, Straus and Giroux
18 West 18th Street, New York 10011

Copyright © 2009 by David Thomson
Printed in the United States of America
Originally published in 2009 by Penguin Books, Great Britain
Published in the United States by Faber and Faber, Inc.
First American edition, 2010

Library of Congress Cataloging-in-Publication Data
Thomson, David, 1941–
    Ingrid Bergman / David Thomson ; photo research by Lucy Gray. —
1st American ed.
        p.   cm.— (Great stars)
    ISBN: 978-0-86547-934-0 (pbk. : alk. paper)
    1. Bergman, Ingrid, 1915–1982.   2. Actors—Sweden—Biography.
I. Title.

PN2778.B43T46 2010
791.4302'8092—dc22
[B]

2009041757

www.fsgbooks.com

1 3 5 7 9 10 8 6 4 2

INGRID BERGMAN

Around the middle of the twentieth century, the advances in photography and self-knowledge came together in a generation of people who loved to be photographed, but who may have confused the process with love itself. Take Ingrid Bergman.

The crucial film was called *Intermezzo*, and the first version, the Swedish, was released in 1936. It is the story of a celebrated concert violinist, Holger Brandt (Gösta Ekman, forty-six at the time), a married man with children. He discovers a new accompanist, Anita Hoffman (Ingrid Bergman, twenty-one). Perhaps it is the force of spring storms melting the winter ice, perhaps it is just their rapport when playing the theme from *Intermezzo* together. They fall rapturously in love and the burnished, aching face of Ingrid Bergman beholds her own glory and her shame – she becomes prettier in love (this mutation is inescapable) and yet she foresees the ignominy of an adulterous affair that even in up-to-date Sweden threatens social order and the rules of the game. At the level of melodrama, the dilemma is posed, and it will never go away – what is an artist to do with life? Anita Hoffman plays discreet and obedient piano backgrounds to the male soloist she loves, but there is no getting away from the pulse of her own creative aspirations. She wants to be in love and to be glorious and, whatever the obstacles or difficulties, she whispers to herself, 'Courage, courage!' Ingrid Bergman is the embodiment of brave discovery: we fall into her face just as she slips away from guilt or friction in the lovely glide of being seen – recognized.

Gösta Ekman is very good in *Intermezzo*, and it is a film about the male character. He has the spiritual egotism of a lofty artist, but he looks haunted, too, by his love for Anita. Ekman and Ingrid were close. They had worked together several times and Ingrid in her diary had talked of marrying Ekman's son (who was her age) as the next best thing. Yet it's clear which man she worshipped, and it's easy to imagine the warmth between them. Gösta gave her bouquets of carnations after *Intermezzo* and told her she was on her way. She even doubted that she could act without him. But in January 1938, he died, and the desperate look on his face became easier to understand. A woman like Ingrid Bergman had to learn early that men were going to fall in love with her, and give off that same hopeless look you see in fading flowers.

At 230 Park Avenue, in those days in the building that housed the New York offices of Selznick International Pictures, there was a Swedish elevator operator, and he very likely knew that the important person at SIP – apart from Mr Selznick and his partner, Mr Whitney – was

Kay Brown. Ms Brown was a small, busy, brown-haired woman, with an inquisitive, friendly smile and a great deal on her mind. But the elevator operator thought he would tell her nevertheless, and just in the time it took to go up and down he mentioned this Swedish film with the lovely girl. The picture was called *Intermezzo*. 'Really?' said Kay Brown, like someone who was always being offered hot tips, but who had learned long ago that you never could tell.

'*Intermezzo*,' said the operator again. 'You have to see this picture. The girl!'

In time, Kay Brown would tell the girl herself the story of the Swedish elevator operator, and the girl smiled, as if confirming the idea that life was like a movie where you could be several thousand miles away, absolutely unaware, as something was happening that might determine your life or change its direction. 'That's lovely!' the girl told Kay Brown.

'Maybe so,' said Ms Brown, 'but you're the lovely one.'

And Ingrid Bergman gave Kay her best smile, that terrific knockout glow that worked just as well life-size as it did on a screen thirty feet high. Here was the thing about Ingrid Bergman: what you got on the screen was there in life. You didn't have to do anything but turn it loose, and let life do the rest. And Ingrid's smile flowered, to think that life could be so generous.

But in Stockholm, in 1939, when Kay Brown had flown there in a small plane in the snows to meet the

Swedish actress, still the American had wondered about her own job. She was a talent scout and what she saw was amazing raw talent. But Ingrid Bergman seemed happy with her husband and a new baby. Kay Brown made the offer, as was her job – to invite Ms Bergman to come to America. But she was wary. She got Ingrid on her own and she said, 'You know, you've got a lovely home and a lovely baby. If I were you I would think it over very carefully.'

But Ingrid was sure. 'Well,' she said, 'if there are people as nice as you in America and in Hollywood, then I'm sure I shall like it, so I shall go, and take the risk.'

So she went, leaving her husband and the eight-month-old baby. There was another pleasant surprise in the discussions. Selznick International would fly her to America. She wouldn't have to swim!

The above may catch you unawares. It is something with which you will have had very little experience – it is an Ingrid Bergman joke. Now, I don't mean to suggest that the story I've just told is hostile to her, much less that it puts her in a false or an unkind light. It's just that I am suggesting that Ingrid Bergman had a calling, allied to a gravitational attraction, and a will that was not to be resisted. She had to act, and see most of the things that happened to her as moments in the act. Thus, with even a younger child in hand, she would have volunteered herself as someone who might swim and walk from Stockholm to Los Angeles if it meant a better opportunity to act. This was in no way mercenary. As we shall see, for several years she was ruthlessly exploited by her owner. Yet she hardly noticed the money. She worked for love of the job, for her soul.

Stories, or fiction-like events, happened to Ingrid Bergman – it was as if life was doing its best to rise to her great desire, or need. For example, she made the journey with Kay Brown in the spring of 1939 as her Europe waited for war. She got to New York, and then she took the train across country. And so she came to Los Angeles, to Beverly Hills, and Kay Brown took her up to the Selznick house on Summit Drive on a Sunday morning.

When they got there, Irene Selznick was sitting on the lawn of the great house listening to the broadcast of a horse race on the radio. Ingrid waited patiently until it was over. And then Irene Selznick greeted her and welcomed her and explained that her husband – Mr Selznick – was at the studio where, even on a Sunday, they were making something called *Gone With the Wind*.

'Where is your luggage?' asked Mrs Selznick, and Ingrid indicated just the one suitcase she had put down at the edge of the lawn.

So she was shown her room at the Selznick house and Irene said that Ingrid should accompany her that evening on a social engagement. She was having dinner at the Beachcomber restaurant with Grace Moore, Miriam Hopkins and Richard Barthelmess. Ingrid was to come along, too. And Mr Selznick? Ingrid asked. Oh, he'll be by.

She went to the restaurant where she rather intimidated Richard Barthelmess by towering over him. And
then they all went back to Miriam Hopkins' house. It
got to be one o'clock in the morning and Ingrid was
dozing, when someone told her that Mr Selznick was in
the kitchen. He was at the table, stuffing himself with
food. He looked up and saw her height, he groaned and
said, 'God! Take your shoes off.' He studied her and
said her name was impossible. It sounded German. Perhaps they'd use her husband's name – 'Lindstrom.'

The young Swedish woman said, no, that was not
possible – 'That's the name I was born with and people
will have to learn to pronounce it.'

Selznick sighed and turned to other things that might
be more easily managed: her eyebrows, her teeth, her
make-up – she needed a lot of work.

At this, Ingrid Bergman told her boss, 'I think you've
made a big mistake, Mr Selznick. You shouldn't have
bought the pig in the sack. I thought you saw me in the
movie *Intermezzo*, and liked me, and sent Kay Brown
across to Sweden to get me. Now you've seen me, you
want to change everything. So I'd rather not do the
movie. We'll say no more about it. No trouble of any
kind. We'll just forget it. I'll take the next train and go
back home.'

There are ways of interpreting that scene: Selznick
was exhausted, eating to get fuel, while she had had the
advantage of a nap. Or that she sized him up immediately as a gambler, and called him. It would be a part of

With David O. Selznick

that reading that she guessed at Selznick's chronic weakness, his habit of second-guessing himself, and knew
that if she stayed firm and resolute he would be eating
out of her hand. If. If? If Ingrid Bergman had it, by
force of will and nature, if she had such an immediately
likeable personality and such an untouched, natural
starriness that any compromise was stupid. And she
had to be liked for herself. So he envisaged the package
over Miriam Hopkins' kitchen table. He took her at her
own word and saw that time and again this towering
young woman from Sweden was going to tell her own
story, and succeed or fail on the strength of her bold
honesty. You didn't flatter this one by telling her you
loved her and sending her flowers and paying her the
earth. You had to love her. So let her have her way –
take the easy way out. If only he'd had the good sense
then and there to let her great emotional energy rescue
him. If only he'd seen that his part in her play was to
yield, to agree, to be hers – it might have been the saving of David O. Selznick, even before *Gone With the
Wind* opened. Still, he went as far as he could.

The very next day, taking Ingrid around his studio,
introducing her and putting his first spin on her, he said,
'I've got an idea that's so simple and yet no one in Hollywood has ever tried it before. Nothing about you is
going to be touched. Nothing altered. You remain yourself. You are going to be the first "natural" actress.'

Ingrid breaks into the most radiant smile anyone in
America has seen yet – a smile like the first time she

ever saw her daughter Pia. And this is the moment when some sour comedian telling the story might add, 'And Ingrid Bergman looks at him, and says "OK, then, you can call me Rumpelstiltskin!"'

There are actors and actresses with unhappy childhoods – or with stories of their own upbringing that seem to beg for sympathy and understanding. It is hard, in fact, to find a life more disturbed than that of Ingrid Bergman's. But do not expect any great song of loneliness or deprivation from Ingrid herself. In the photographs that survive she seems to shine with confidence as much as she gives off the lounging air of health and vitality. Her early years had been filled with loss and uncertainty. An ordinary person might have become convinced of her own misfortune or unhappiness. But Ingrid Bergman seems to have taken it all in her large stride. After all, it was not quite so much that she was destined to be a person, as an actress. Now an actress cannot have too much happening to her. She collects imagined experiences and other types like a boy steaming stamps off envelopes. A time will come when she may be the greatest actress in the world in scenes of distress, inner misery, heartfelt confession and being a natural victim. But the woman who could convey that turmoil seldom weakened or cracked in herself. She was a warrior. We must not forget that she was half German.

Her mother was Friedel Adler, from Hamburg. As a young woman, Friedel had visited Sweden (there are regular ferries from Hamburg to Stockholm) and she had met Justus Samuel Bergman. The story was that she met Justus walking in the woods and coming on a glade where he was painting. He was thirteen years older than Friedel but they fell in love and wanted to marry. The Adlers were not excited: Justus was Swedish; he was too old; and he did too little. So he stopped painting and opened a photography shop in Stockholm – in his own pictures, he is an amusing, small-featured man, dark, humorous, with a teasing glance into the camera. But he was respectable enough now to be married, and on 29 August 1915 Ingrid was born in Stockholm. When the child was 3, Friedel died of liver disease. Ingrid hardly recalled her except as a figure in photographs, or in the stories told by her father.

Of course, she grew closer to her father. She loved being in his shop, and she enjoyed it when he showed her the old love letters written by Friedel. Every year, Justus took his daughter to Hamburg to visit that side of their family. And whenever possible, the father indulged Ingrid's fascination with acting. Her paternal aunt, Aunt Ellen, took over the mother's role, but she was not in favour of Justus's lifestyle and she warned them both that all this play-acting was the devil's work. There were evenings when Justus had several people to dinner and, during the meal, Ingrid would act out all the roles in a story. Justus hired a nanny, a teenage girl, Greta, to help look after Ingrid – and then he fell in love with Greta. They might have married, but Justus developed cancer. He died when Ingrid was still only 12 years old.

After the death of Justus Ingrid lived with Aunt Ellen – with the result, not much more than six months later, that the aunt died in the niece's arms.

Ingrid moved in with her Uncle Otto and Aunt Hulda – it was a large family, with many more relatives left. All of them disapproved of Ingrid's desire to enter the theatre. These were strict Lutheran Protestants who held the theatre in disdain, the more so because in most conventional respects Ingrid was not a good student or one who seemed to be trying hard. But it's a measure of Ingrid's ability and confidence that she had a private acting instructress and a personal gymnastics instructor when she was still in her teens. She said she was a lonely girl, and that must have been so, but others reckoned she was pampered and even spoiled. No matter the opposition, she was used to getting her own way when her most intense performance was that of the girl who wanted to go to drama school. No one close to her had any doubt about her destiny and her ability, or about their sense that she was already in her element.

She would audition at the Royal Dramatic Theatre in Stockholm. In a country as small and organized as Sweden it was the only way to go: Greta Gustafson had had a scholarship there in 1922–24 and she had become Greta Garbo. She was in Los Angeles now, one of the most famous women in movies, a face that spelled out the new rapture that existed between great beauties and millions of strangers. As for Ingrid, she thought the movies were all very well, but it was the stage that drew her on. Her father had talked about her singing in opera. But there was one sympathetic uncle, Gunnar, who talked of the stage. So she dreamed of being a new Bernhardt. But she was laughed at: she was so shy, so awkward! 'I couldn't come into a room without bumping into the furniture and then blushing . . . Since those days I've discovered that many actors and actresses are like this – extremely shy people. When they're acting, they're not themselves; they're somebody else – the other people they're pretending to be are responsible for the words coming out of their mouth.'

So one day in 1933 she was one of seventy-five novices who tried out at the Royal Dramatic Theatre for eight places. She was tall, a little plump, she was shy and bashful – or she was huge, radiant and a certainty. Let's allow she was both. She had leaped onto the stage as the mad boy in Rostand's *L'Aiglon*. She felt no one was paying attention. As she finished there was silence. But she was chosen. A few days later she met Alf Sjöberg, a director at the Royal Dramatic and one of those who had been testing her. 'The silence when I finished!' said Ingrid. 'I felt so sad.' Sjöberg smiled, and he said, 'We didn't have to talk about it. Your assurance, your security! We knew.' The judges also noted, as she did a scene from Strindberg, that she had a natural, country look. She did not seem like a conventional actress. Of course, that is acting's greatest trick, and she had it by the scruff of the neck.

As far as anyone can tell, Ingrid Bergman had had not so much as a boyfriend before Petter Lindstrom. She was unusually tall. She was utterly preoccupied with her acting. She had a theory worked out that she hated men and could do without them. But then one day she was drawn into a blind date foursome. He was a man of the world, tall and handsome, a practising dentist, with a car of his own. He seemed a lot older. But he invited her to lunch and then they went cross-country skiing together. He was eight and a half years older than she was. He was taller than she was and was a natural athlete as well as an outstanding dancer. He was good-looking and he was close to perfect if you could ignore that slight edge of arrogance or over-confidence. He was relaxed with the pretty acting student, but there was a controlling side to him. It was just that she was willing to be led for the while by a man who knew so much more than she did – except in matters of the imagination, impulse, motivation and cunning. But you can't have everything.

He came from a northern village, Stode, and that's where he'd learned all his sports as well as a taste for journeys to Lappland. But he was a remarkable figure in that he had also become a friend to many people in the arts in Stockholm. He was destined to become one of the more infamous cuckolds in twentieth-century history, but he was a talented and thoughtful man, and he

was certainly one of those who best understood Ingrid
Bergman, even if he had so many good reasons for
resenting her and mistrusting her. It's not just that he
became her first husband, and the father of her first
child. In addition, he was a very useful adviser to her
and was nearly her agent in the early years of her
career.

But the career was begun, and determined on, before
Petter appeared. Before she had encountered the young
dentist, she had made *Swedenhielms* – indeed, she was
only 19, carrying a little more puppy fat than we are
used to, when Gustaf Molander cast her in that film.
Molander was a veteran, nearly 50, experienced but
neglected just because his work stayed Swedish. Yet
Swedenhielms is a remarkable picture, a bubbly comedy
that turns suddenly sombre – it's a shift of mood worthy of Renoir or Ingmar Bergman. So Ingrid Bergman
had made a very good film years before *Casablanca*.

The title refers to a family made up of a rather cheer-
fully mad scientist (Gösta Ekman), his housekeeper and
his three children. It's a well-to-do household, with this
proviso: nearly everyone is always borrowing money
from someone else. The chief culprit is Bobby, an air
force pilot, whose girlfriend is Astrid (Ingrid Bergman).
The mounting debt is real, yet it's treated comically,
with the running joke that, 'It'll be all right when Dad
wins the Nobel Prize!' This high-spirited household is a
little reminiscent of some Frank Capra set-ups – the
giddy whirl only just masks deeper issues. Molander

may have known his Capra, but he was also part of a
Swedish tradition – of rigorous social analyses lit up by
the spirit of comedy. *Swedenhielms* isn't just an oddity, it's
a sophisticated, screwball film about human groups and
interior space where the camera makes subtle movements and the blocking of action is more developed
than it would have been in Hollywood in 1935. And
Ekman is hilarious and tender, not least in that moment
when he takes a hurried phone call and hears that he
has won that prize!

This was only Ingrid's third film, and her part is not
of major size. But when we see her first, in recline,
laughing and giggling on the telephone, the film seems
to know what a treasure it has. Molander was apparently taken with the big girl immediately. He shot a test
and told her to do nothing in it – just be photographed.
The next day at the rushes, Ingrid complained, 'I didn't
look very good, did I? I could do better.' But Molander
hushed her. He knew she had no need to do more. He
would make six films with her before she left Sweden,
and if Molander had only made that big trip with her he
might have been an important figure in America of the
1940s.

There isn't time now to explore the detail of *Swedenhielms*, but it's still there to be seen. Ingrid was as
impressed with Ekman as with Molander and it's plain
that both men adored her and took on the task of
schooling her. So she loses weight in the next couple of
years and she learns to laugh less. With Ingrid Bergman's

smile, the laugh is entirely unnecessary. You can see the progress made in both *Intermezzo* and *Dollar*, which is another fast comedy of talk and manners, concerning flirtatious couples on holiday, and giving Ingrid the chance to show that she spoke better English than Elsa Burnett (an American actress living in Sweden who also appears in the film).

As for Ekman, 'He gave me little tips and I was in heaven. My happiness cannot be described when he said later, "You are really very talented. I like you very much. You help me to play because your face and expressions reflect every word I say." . . . I wonder if he feels how my eyes follow him like a dog's. I adore him more than ever.'

The mere existence of *Intermezzo* suggests how much was noticed, for the story of the film is that of the sea-soned virtuoso who realizes that he has stumbled upon a fellow-artist so talented that he must soon need and love her. To watch the Swedish version of the film is to see a love story being enacted. Perhaps Petter noticed, too – for Ingrid and Gösta did not work together again after the marriage. Nevertheless for any Swede – includ-ing the elevator operator at 230 Park Avenue – the orig-inal *Intermezzo* was regarded as a Gösta Ekman picture. Moreover, Ekman in the Swedish version seems like a man torn apart by his illicit love affair whereas Leslie Howard in the Selznick remake is a sedate fellow whose pipe feels as important to him as his violin.

But Ingrid did more still in the years between the two

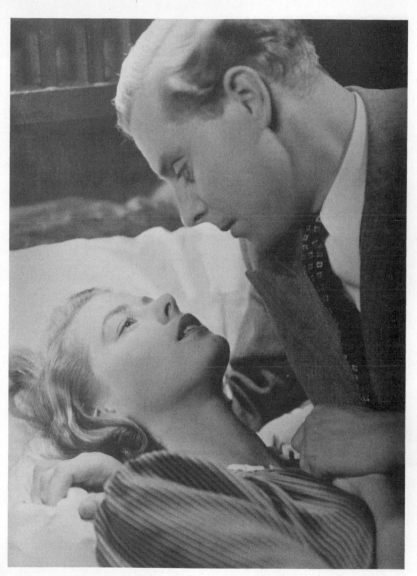

In *Intermezzo* with Gösta Ekman

*Intermezzo*s. In 1938 (for Molander again), she appeared in *A Woman's Face*, playing a young woman whose face has been disfigured. (This story was remade a few years later, at MGM, with George Cukor directing and with Joan Crawford in the lead.) Ingrid played the disfigured woman, and she recruited dentist Petter to remake her mouth to fit the make-up scarring. Her character is transformed by plastic surgery, of course, but she is haunted by a blackmailing figure from her past, and she kills him. No Bergman character had behaved as forcefully or as melodramatically. Molander himself was uncertain how to end the film, and it was Ingrid herself who rejected any specious happy ending, deciding that the woman goes to trial, with the audience left in suspense as to the verdict.

Something else happened that would fade away later as the publicity machine at Selznick smoothed out her life. Ingrid had not given up the German side of her family. Petter – a sturdy anti-Fascist – had been alarmed when he went with his new wife to Hamburg and observed that she joined in the Heil Hitlering with enthusiasm, or at least with automatic acceptance. Later on, Ingrid would say that this was not so – she had found herself at a Nazi Party rally and been taken aback by all the saluting. A German companion had told her, you just join in, but Ingrid had declined because she was Swedish.

In fact, she was half German and she spoke German as well as she did English. And at this point in her life she seems to have found UFA, the German production company, as her most promising way ahead. In 1938, she actually signed a three-picture deal with UFA and *The Four Companions* was its first result. It was a light comedy directed by Carl Fröhlich, but it was made and Ingrid spent a good deal of time in the Nazi country without apparent strain. Indeed, there was even a rumour that she was about to be invited to tea by Dr Goebbels when Petter's strenuous efforts got her back to Sweden and made her available for the remake of *Intermezzo*.

The shooting on *Intermezzo* began in late May 1939 – more or less as David O. Selznick drew near the projected end of scheduled shooting on *Gone With the Wind*. Of course, that project shattered every schedule, so that the modest Swedish romance came along sheltered by the boss's helpless concentration on a far bigger project. In Hollywood, the story had every advantage: William Wyler was the first director hired, with Harry Stradling doing the photography. Leslie Howard, as he finished Ashley Wilkes, would play the great violinist. He was also credited as executive producer, which seemed to allow him some directorial say on the romantic scenes. But Selznick could not leave well enough alone.

After a few days, Wyler was dismissed and replaced with Gregory Ratoff. Few directors were so far apart: Wyler was cautious, a realist, a naturalist building his films slowly – Ratoff was a hammy actor, a melodrama man, with a very thick Russian accent so that his line readings for Ingrid were frequently a source of comedy on set. In theory, Ratoff was all wrong, but the film came through, even if it is inferior to the Swedish production. A more crucial change saw Harry Stradling being replaced as photographer by Gregg Toland to get an ideal way of shooting Ingrid. In Sweden, a lot of high-key work had been used with Ingrid. Selznick now saw that her face responded to more shadow and a softer, longer hairstyle. He tried to hide her height and he gave strict orders to Toland on no shooting from the rear – Ingrid never had the greatest figure. But Toland – who would do *Citizen Kane* the following year, and who was never known for his glamour work – began to discover a more desirable Ingrid Bergman. Beyond that, I think it's fair to say that Howard's reticence – or superiority – makes the violinist seem a shade less involved than was the case with Gösta Ekman. In the second *Intermezzo*, the young woman is the more active character, and Bergman stole the picture visually.

The Selznick post-production cut *Intermezzo* down from nearly two hours to seventy minutes, and the picture had several promising previews. It opened in October 1939 at Radio City Music Hall (two months before *Gone With the Wind*), and it went from shooting to being finished in less than five months. Ingrid was a hit but she was not at her own premiere. In August (just after doing some Technicolor screen tests for Selznick), and just before the Nazi invasion of Poland, she was whisked

off back to Sweden, filled with advice from Selznick
not to get further involved with the German movie
business. Selznick was in suspense about another matter, of course: the success or failure of *Gone With the
Wind* would alter his life. He was confident about Ingrid,
but he was not yet sure how to handle her and he showed
no sign of being in love with her. He was ready to risk
losing her. Apparently, just like the young woman in
Intermezzo, Ingrid was ready to go home to her family,
even if home was in a neutral country very close to the
source of conflict in a world war. In *Intermezzo*, the girl
moves on, confident that her courage will bring her further opportunities. But Ingrid may have been more
wary.

Her young daughter hardly recognized her. The
preparations for war were very serious. The word was
that *Intermezzo* had done nicely (though not so well in
the provinces), but *Gone With the Wind* was an industry unto itself. Vivien Leigh was the clear star and sensation at Selznick's studio, and if he had a new picture in
mind – *Rebecca* – that was one that required a young English actress, a wallflower, not a tall plant like Ingrid.
She wrote to her old friends in Hollywood, most nota-
bly her trusted dialogue coach, Ruth Roberts, and in her
memory she built up the treatment she had had from
David Selznick: 'I trusted him when we saw the rushes
and to everything he thought. His judgment was very
hard but it was just. To work for him is often terribly
demanding and very hard on the nerves. But always

there is the feeling that you have somebody to help with
understanding, encouragement and wisdom, and that is
beyond price. When I left, he asked me to sign an enormous photograph, and I wrote "For David, I have no
words, Ingrid." Which is true.'

At the same time, Ingrid was now 24: she had been
given her shot and sent home – of course she agreed, she
had a baby at home waiting for her. In fact, by 1940,
she had made twelve films and clearly demonstrated her
ability in comedy and romance. She was also a ravenous
learner, picking up so much craft and assurance in the
Selznick venture. In fact, Selznick never tested Ingrid
for *Rebecca* (tests went to Vivien Leigh, Loretta Young,
Margaret Sullavan and Joan Fontaine), but if he had,
Bergman would have excelled in the part. She was too
tall, maybe, but that could be handled. More important,
she could do emotional shyness with stunning expert-
ise. Joan Fontaine is superb in *Rebecca* but I think Ingrid
would have been as good – and surely the new Mrs de
Winter could have been made Swedish without too
much trouble. Yet Selznick did not think of it.

He admired Ingrid Bergman, for her beauty and intelligence and for the very unusual blend of the two. He
could teach her and talk to her and it's hard to believe he
didn't make a pass at her – that was a conscientious part
of his art and his trade. It was said at the Selznick studio
if you made a pass at Ingrid she became cross or vexed,
because it was a departure from professionalism and
a waste of her time. But that concentration did ease.

Ingrid was susceptible, and she was shrewd enough to know where availability could work. In a year, Selznick would meet another actress – Phyllis Isley (after she had been noticed by Kay Brown). He would change her name to Jennifer Jones. He would make her his cause and his life, his star actress and his insecure wife, yet surely he knew in his bones that Ingrid was far superior as an actress and as a screen force. He had Ingrid under contract, but in the seven years of that deal she would make only two films for him directly – *Intermezzo* and *Spellbound*. Ships that pass in the crowded night. It is one of the most intriguing 'if onlys' in Hollywood history.

Selznick did ask her to come back – the chance to play St Joan was the bait. Ingrid, Petter and Pia travelled by train to Genoa, passing through Berlin on the way, and then took a ship from Genoa to New York. (Another passenger on the ship was Martha Gellhorn who wrote to Ernest Hemingway to say how impressive Ingrid was.) Alas, once the actress landed in New York the first thing she was told by Selznick's agents was to suspend the St Joan talk – that project was on hold.

Ingrid's contract with Selznick International was for one picture, *Intermezzo*, at $25,000, and then two more – rising to $40,000 a picture. But at the same time, Ingrid was free to do a couple of pictures a year in other countries, if the opportunity arose. But then at Selznick's prodding, she had terminated her arrangement with UFA. So what would she do? In just a few years' time,

Ingrid Bergman would be more in demand than any actress in sight. By 1945, she was in the top ten box-office attractions and comedians could get a laugh by saying, 'I saw a picture last night – and Ingrid Bergman wasn't in it!' Yet 1940–41 was a strange hiatus, prompted by Selznick's personal uncertainty (he was close to having a breakdown) and his urge to hire his contract players out to other studios instead of making use of them himself. It was a period in which Ingrid became more frustrated and thus more authoritative. She was put in a position, she felt, where she had to take charge herself. Courage, courage!

In the hiatus, Ingrid was kept out of two intriguing films, she did a play in New York, and she made two films as poor as anything she would ever do. One actor who had been very impressed with her was Fredric March, a man who had worked for Selznick. He tried to get Ingrid to be the female lead in two of his pictures, both directed by John Cromwell: *Victory*, from the Conrad novel, and *So Ends Our Night*, from a novel by Erich Maria Remarque. Nothing came of the attempt – Betty Field got the part in *Victory* and Margaret Sullavan in *So Ends Our Night*. Neither picture did very well, but in both cases the mood of the film was tragic – so that one can imagine Ingrid doing quite well.

But she did get the female lead, opposite Burgess Meredith, in a Broadway run of *Liliom*, the Ferenc Molnar play that is also the basis of *Carousel*. Benno

Schneider directed the play and Ingrid got positive notices without ever creating a sensation.

And then she was loaned away, to Columbia for *Adam Had Four Sons*, directed by one of her least favourite people, Gregory Ratoff, and to Metro-Goldwyn-Mayer for *Rage in Heaven*, directed by Woody Van Dyke (and co-starring Robert Montgomery and George Sanders). It would be possible to see just these two films and conclude that the actress – one Ingrid Bergman – came and went like so many Continental actresses, without leaving a lasting impression. No matter the care and attention Selznick had paid to *Intermezzo*, he could not find better material for her at first, and so he seems to have let these minor films be made without much intervention or protest. If you want the full measure of his neglect, then you have only to say that her next two movies were stunning pieces of work that to this day secure her reputation, *Dr Jekyll and Mr Hyde* and *Casablanca*.

Something else happened in this period. The Bergmans were often separated. Petter was sometimes in Sweden and then sometimes at the University of Rochester where he had decided to pursue American medical studies so that he would be free to practise in the United States. This was a mark of his seriousness and diligence, but it was also a dangerous liberty. Ingrid was a modest star by now, doing things on radio, being taken to parties and meeting people. It is the time in which she seemed to develop the capacity of falling in love with other people.

One of those was the director Victor Fleming. It seems clear that as Fleming and Selznick laboured and often battled to complete *Gone With the Wind* in the summer of 1939, the director at least saw the Technicolor tests done by Ingrid Bergman before she went back to Sweden. He was impressed by them. He may have met Ingrid. By 1941, he was preparing to do a remake of Stevenson's *Dr Jekyll and Mr Hyde* – a remake in that the outstanding and pioneering Rouben Mamoulian version from 1932 loomed over the project. That was the film where Fredric March had won the Oscar in transformation scenes that surpassed explanation. In addition, that first sound version of the great story had stressed the ordinary sexual content in the myth, the struggle between libido and repression. Miriam Hopkins had been very good in that 1932 film playing the sluttish character, Ivy, who brings out the beast in Jekyll.

We don't know enough about what prompted the MGM remake in 1941, except that it was seen from the start as a vehicle for Spencer Tracy. It was the actor's wish to play the two parts with as much psychological realism and as few special effects as possible. There was a screenplay, by John Lee Mahin (a Fleming regular), that begins with a very strong scene in a church on Sunday. The preacher is talking about good and evil, when one of the congregation (played by the considerable actor Barton MacLane) bursts out with 'give evil a chance'. He has to be led away, and through the agency of another person in the church, Dr Henry Jekyll, he is taken to a madhouse. But Jekyll himself has been most impressed by the insurgent's cry. As the man is taken away, Jekyll insists on kissing his fiancée (the young Lana Turner) full on the lips in public, and then he playfully nibbles at her knuckles. The girl's father (Donald Crisp) is shocked at this glimpse of sensuality and he worries all the more as he hears Jekyll's thesis about the faint line that separates good and evil in all people – and their need to have the evil or sensual side given expression.

This originality is beyond the range of Mahin's other scripts, and it seems a big reach for Fleming. So perhaps the picture was driven forward by Tracy, a man who had separate sides to his personality – the drunk and the sober, and two not quite as distinct – the straight and the gay. I propose this not in any spirit of gossip (Tracy is still vehemently defended as double straight by some) but because the depth and tone of *Dr Jekyll and Mr Hyde* have to be explained.

As written, Mahin's script calls for two female roles: Beatrix, Jekyll's fiancée, and Ivy, the girl Hyde encounters at night on the streets. For years the story has been told how Ingrid, hearing of the project, and being talked about for the film, manoeuvred a casting change so that she got the part of Ivy, instead of Beatrix. Now, let's be clear, she could have played either woman – or both (which may be the most intriguing way of going). Ingrid herself, in *My Life*, states categorically that Fleming did a secret screen test with herself as Ivy and used that to persuade Selznick, and then switched Lana Turner to the role of Beatrix. But in his recent biography of Victor Fleming, Michael Sragow reports studio documents that had Ingrid pencilled in as Ivy from the outset, and long before Turner was talked about.

The matter has been inflated in that, a few years later, Fleming would become one of Ingrid's lovers – but no one seems to think he had fallen for her before the making of *Jekyll and Hyde*. (Anyone might have fallen for her during the filming, however.) So the secret screen test builds the pact between the actress and the director, unless it is all a pipe dream that helps us realize that Ingrid Bergman might say anything on her own behalf. Another biographer of Ingrid, Laurence Leamer, adds that Selznick knew about the screen test and may even have attended it.

The factual confusion falls aside once one starts to see the film. Ivy is not quite the whorish figure Miriam Hopkins had played in 1932. She's a bar-girl, cheerful, open, sexy and eager to live life to the full – indeed, she serves at first to help lure Jekyll out of his self-imposed repression. But there follows a long scene between the two of them that seems to me more suggestive and sophisticated than anything Fleming and Mahin ever did, and which is the first great piece of film in Ingrid Bergman's career. She has been injured in a modest way and he is her doctor. But this is all a seduction, too, in which she draws him into a fatal kiss that triggers Hyde's

With Spencer Tracy in *Dr Jekyll and Mr Hyde*

emergence (or erection). It is shot largely in close-up
and it relies on innuendo in the dialogue and superb
control and underplaying. If I say this, that Tracy and
Bergman seem nearly breathless with each other, then
maybe that needs to be trusted: maybe the two of them
worked out the scene and became very close because of
it. Or maybe Fleming fell for Ingrid as he saw her coming to life – a life of his making – before his eyes.

It is a great meeting scene, and in the line of history,
a startling demonstration of how much Ingrid had
learned (or of how much she had always possessed by
instinct). In truth, she dictates the scene – even though
she is Hyde's victim, truly afraid of his released, sadistic
demon, and quite candid in hinting at the kinds of bru-
tality he has been practising on her. I find it easy to think
that Tracy and Fleming fell for her as the work pro-
ceeded – these are scenes of uncommon erotic tension,
enough to lift the film clear of all the set-piece clichés
that by now attend Jekyll and Hyde. Other observers
felt that it was all a display of Ingrid's power and a demonstration of how easily she could take over a picture.
By contrast, in the film as a whole, Lana Turner comes
off like a buttercup put beside Ingrid's bloody roses.

Above all, the scenes established the impression that
Ingrid Bergman was far more than just a sweet, virtuous, 'natural' Swedish girl – she was a dark sensualist
over whom many men might go mad. Her very image
delivered a climate of adult romantic expectation. She
was the sort of woman who might make men forget the

existence of war. She surely knew something of what had been achieved. *Dr Jekyll and Mr Hyde* may not have been the most comfortable of sets. Its degree of psychological insight was years ahead of its time, and it would be a long time before the world realized that Tracy and Ingrid had delivered not just the Stevenson story but a parable about sexual liberty and its dangers.

'I would have paid anything for this picture. Shall I ever be happier in my work? Will I ever get a better part than the little girl Ivy Petersen, a better director than Victor Fleming, a more wonderful leading man than Spencer Tracy, and a better cameraman than Joe Ruttenberg? I have never been happier. Never have I given myself so completely. For the first time I have broken out from the cage which encloses me, and opened a shutter to the outside world. I have touched things which I hoped were there but I have never dared to show. I am so happy for this picture. It is as if I were flying. I feel no chains. I can fly higher and higher because the bars of my cage are broken.'

In the beginning, when it was just a play called *Everybody Comes to Rick's*, the girl was American and she was named Lois Meredith. She was an American adventuress who had had an affair with Rick in Paris, and been unfaithful to him. So that had broken them up until Casablanca when she walked into Rick's Café again and heard Sam playing and singing 'As Time Goes By'. So Warner Brothers looked quickly at the treatments they had and guessed that it would be one of their regular actors – George Raft, maybe – with Ann Sheridan.

But Hal Wallis, the decisive executive in charge of the project, was certain that it was material for a new Humphrey Bogart, who had recently appeared in *The Maltese Falcon*. And as the play was gradually turned into a script – with the work of the Epstein brothers, Howard Koch, Casey Robinson and Wallis himself – so Lois changed into Ilsa. Casey Robinson took credit for it because he said he was in love with a Russian ballerina, Tamara Toumanova, at the time – he even thought she could play the part. But Ilsa was a rather nicer girl than Lois had been – if a little harder to believe in. Ilsa was married to Victor Laszlo a freedom fighter, but she thought Victor was dead and that's how she had the affair with Rick in Paris. Then she learned that Laszlo was alive and that's when honour redirected her part. But still, she and Victor come to Casablanca looking for an escape, only to find that Rick runs the show.

Wallis wanted a foreign actress who could speak good English. He looked at Edwige Feuillère, at Michèle Morgan, and Hedy Lamarr. There are always casting lists in the files full of names that might be OK, but which don't mean that anyone was ever asked. But as Ilsa became Ilsa Lund, it was harder to believe that Wallis was thinking of anyone except Ingrid Bergman. Of course, from Wallis's point of view that meant dealing with David Selznick, so he sent the Epsteins to tell Selznick the story of the picture. They got him over lunch and they went into the background, the kind of place Casablanca was, and had hardly mentioned Ilsa, when Selznick said they could have her. Kay Brown called Ingrid with the news in Rochester and the actress was so eager and impatient she couldn't sleep. For fear of waking Petter, she got up, and started walking around their apartment, thinking of herself as Ilsa Lund, but having very little idea as yet what the film was about.

When Ingrid turned up at Warners and met her likely director on the film, Michael Curtiz, she asked as was her way, what was she to be? Curtiz waved any doubts aside. Be Ingrid Bergman, he said. But what is that? she asked, just like one of the public, little realizing how far *Casablanca* would clear the matter up for eternity. It's not that *Casablanca* was a minor project for Warners, but no one – from Hal Wallis or Michael Curtiz down – had any reliable notion of what it would be. It was a war picture, obviously, and war was the pressing subject. But war had imposed economies at every studio. We are embarking on one of the handful of archetypal Hollywood films, but we don't know that yet. For the moment it is just another production where the script is being reworked. If Bergman asks Curtiz which of these two men she will be with at the end of the picture, just tell her very nicely, 'Wait and see!'

The picture was going to cost close to $1 million. The play cost $20,000. The writers were paid $53,000. Curtiz would receive $73,400. Bogart $33,667. Bergman, Paul Henreid and Conrad Veidt got $25,000 each.

Claude Rains got $22,000. There was a studio overhead of more than $223,000. They had to pay for the film stock, the processing and the sets, the lighting crew, the sound team and the builders. They needed letters of transit, an upright piano and at the end a sketch of an airfield where farewells could be made. The only thing not on the budget was the magic.

How did it happen? Well, Bogart was wary of Ingrid. She was bigger than he was and bolder. She led with her strongest feelings and her searching gaze, while he was at his best backing off, as a counter puncher, grinning at her sincerity as if he'd seen everything now. He had had very little experience playing romantic scenes – just try to think of Bogart in a kissing scene before *Casablanca*. So he worked it out that he would wait for her moves. After all, he was a guy and guys were above romance and that silly stuff. He also had had warnings from his tempestuous wife – his third, Mayo Methot – that if he let the big Swede get her hands on him then she would cut him to pieces. So it helped Bogart that Rick had turned savage and morose with self-pity. And as he backed off, she had only to look at him as if she was ready to die. In other words, the ways in which they wanted to be seen began to fit together. And the very daft story of *Casablanca* works its way towards Rick telling Ilsa to shape up, to be a man, to make a few sacrifices here and there. So we know she knows it's Rick she wants, but she's going with Victor for the sake of the war and doing the right thing. What more can a war ask?

With Bogart in *Casablanca*

In other words, if Ingrid Bergman could read the early scripts of *Casablanca* and wonder which man Ilsa was going to go with at the end, then she really didn't yet understand Hollywood pictures. (We should not discount that possibility – it helps explain a lot of her actions.) It could work out another way. A certain kind of Ilsa could tell Rick and the American people after his sanctimonious speech about the hill of beans that she doesn't care about the war effort or the fight against Fascism, she just wants to go south into the desert with Rick to infinite oases of mad love that have given up the ghost on the world, its Big Issues and its bean-counters. Of course, she might notice that Bogart's Rick is hardly the best company – she might have done better with Peter Lorre's Ugarte or even Conrad Veidt's Strasser (there are some of us who see the mad sensualist in him). Rick is going to do his duty because Bogart is intimidated by social pressures. Ilsa is going to do as she's told – and there, I think, we come upon the secret of future adventure in Ingrid Bergman. She was not good at doing what men told her to do.

So Ilsa is the prisoner in *Casablanca*: she is going to have to decide – but the real decision over her liberty is in Rick's hands. He settles it and proves himself war-ready in a decision that was intended to encourage American participation in the war. What *Casablanca* discovers is Ingrid Bergman's profound aptitude for being a prisoner, for feeling torture and the agonies of indecision. If Hal Wallis was as good an executive as I suspect then he teased Ingrid every day with fresh clues about how the story would end. For the emotional commitment of the actress had gone way beyond any thought of common sense in the woman. 'I kissed him,' Bergman would say of Bogie later, 'But I never knew him.' It was her kind of torture.

So what made it work? First of all, the highest skills of a Hollywood studio working at its peak of efficiency, and confident that it could translate the hard-soft flimflam of its tough talk and male dream situations into a lifelike noir romance. That involved silky camera movements, a lustrous control of lighting so that every scene seems to be 'night', a scheme of dialogue in which the action keeps edging forward, and a cast so perfect down to the smallest roles that the world feels bounteous.

Ingrid was still only 27, yet she looks older, sadder, more experienced – the girlishness there even in her Ivy has been replaced by a woman of the world. This comes from her own look, and from the way Arthur Edeson has photographed her. Her blondeness has faded to brown; her eyebrows are going darker and – just as Selznick believed was right – shadow now encroaches on her face to make it seem more vulnerable. Moreover, there is something new: the depth in her eyes, the feeling of earned experience and the lowness of her voice are now as one. The younger Ingrid had giggled and squeaked occasionally. But now the look and the voice are in unison, and the accent is not just gentle but beguiling. It's worth noting that *Casablanca* opened one year after Garbo's last film, *Two-Faced Woman*, but Ingrid's voice sounded friendlier and warmer to American ears than Garbo had ever managed.

So all that Ingrid had on her side was Warner Brothers' brilliance, a few more elegant dresses than a woman on the run in 1942 might have been expected to have, and all the men gazing at her like lamps in the darkness. Moreover, *Casablanca* is a film about wartime uncertainty: it speaks to millions of people who had a man far away or a girl at home – and someone else available now. As a fantasy it indulges the idea of one person with two lovers, an idea that is invariably more dangerous or damaging in life than the dream allows. And finally, Ingrid was the new woman, not just Swedish but a refugee, the category of human being that would be so important after the war and which would then dissolve into the world citizenship of the millennium. Ilsa Lund is an international figure, stateless and far from home, but believing in the world. It was a role that would carry Ingrid off the rails in just a few years.

Then, at the very end, magic came along to give *Casablanca* its lift. The film had been shot in the early summer of 1942. By August, Wallis was running the rough-cut to see whether they needed any Bergman retakes – she had won the part of Maria in *For Whom the Bell Tolls*, and was about to go on location. There was a lot of optimism at the studio that the picture worked. Then, early in November, Allied landings were made on the north African coast between Mehdia and Safi. The central attack had come at a place called Casablanca. The studio was in a daze – it seems unlikely that anyone at Warners had thought to plan a coincidence in the real world, or even knew for sure where Casablanca was. They wondered whether some new footage could be filmed referring to the landings. But it was too late, and so the film ends on the dawn of the beautiful friendship between Rick and Louis. On 26 November the film opened in New York City, and the public swooned to think that movies were so close to life.

Casablanca won the Oscar for Best Picture. Ingrid was not even nominated – though she was in that same year for *For Whom the Bell Tolls*. It didn't matter. When David Selznick saw *Casablanca* he wired Hal Wallis full of congratulation, and concluded, 'Ingrid is obviously going to be what I have for so long predicted. One of the great stars of the world.'

Hemingway's novel of *For Whom the Bell Tolls* was published in October 1940, with a first print of 100,000. It had everything that year needed: not just a clear delineation of the reasons for war, but a story full of adventure and romance. Myron Selznick sold the film rights, to Paramount, for $150,000 and Gary Cooper was immediately under consideration to play the lead, Robert Jordan. Once upon a time, Myron Selznick would have brought the novel for his brother – and clearly that prospect was taken seriously for a moment. But when David Selznick read the book he was convinced that

Maria was a role Ingrid should play. He passed the novel
on to her and, with the aid of a dictionary, she worked
her way through the book. At first, she doubted whether
she could be Spanish, but then she saw a newspaper
story in which Hemingway himself was quoted as saying she was ideal.

In a rush, a meeting was arranged. Ingrid had been
skiing in Sun Valley, while Hemingway was in San Francisco. So Ingrid hurried to meet him for lunch: it was
a reunion with Martha Gellhorn, too, who had met
Ingrid on the boat from Europe. Hemingway told
Ingrid that her hair would need to be cut so he asked to
see her ears. Ingrid did as she was asked and the novelist was charmed. He signed a copy of the book for the
perfect Maria. So then a screen test was done at Paramount where Ingrid wore a short brown wig and slacks,
as suited to the wild life led by Maria. Sam Wood, the
prospective director of the film disliked the test and
said Ingrid was unconvincing. He further demonstrated
his complete unsuitability for the project by deciding
that Maria should be played instead by the German-
Norwegian ballerina, Vera Zorina, who had made a
couple of pictures.

The look of anguish on Ilsa Lund's face owed something to this piece of casting and the possibility that
Ingrid would lose Maria. But as the Hemingway picture
went on location, to the Sierra foothills, so Zorina
proved herself inadequate. Ingrid was doing publicity
pictures with Paul Henreid one day at Warners when

the call came from Selznick to tell her that Zorina was being dropped and that Ingrid would be Maria, opposite Gary Cooper. She was elated, but she was being screwed, too: Paramount paid Selznick over $90,000 on the loan-out, while he gave her her contract salary of nearly $32,000. For the moment, Ingrid seemed not to notice such exploitation, but Petter noticed and was angered. She let her husband do the deals (she had no agent as yet), and he was compelled to haggle over terms on projects where he might expect to be cuckolded, too.

She hurried up to Sonora and gave a vivid account in her autobiography of first seeing Gary Cooper who started talking to her in dialogue from the script. Some onlookers reckoned it was love at first sight. The fact that Cooper was waiting for her was indicative, for he was a past-master of the location romance, and quite capable of getting horny reading the script. After all, Maria, the victim of multiple Fascist rape, was a traumatized woman who would be reclaimed for perfect sex by the tender wooing of Robert Jordan. In Technicolor. And the two of them in the same sleeping bag. America was already a nation of campers, and Hemingway had pioneered some new techniques.

So the Sierra stood in for the Spanish mountains, and a *Casablanca*-like cast of displaced actors filled out the story: Gary Cooper was actually from Montana, where his character had been born; but Ingrid was Swedish, Akim Tamiroff was Russian, Katina Paxinou was

With Cooper in *For Whom the Bell Tolls*

Greek, Joseph Calleia was from Malta, and Vladimir Sokoloff was from the Moscow Art Theatre. *For Whom the Bell Tolls* is a grand, slow picture, far too conscious of its own gravity. Ingrid believed that she had been too crazy about Cooper to look miserable enough as Maria – though she rises to a frenzy of grief at the very end where she is taken away and the wounded Jordan waits to confront the Fascists.

Such a mixture never mattered. In 1943, the film was as sweet to the war effort as *Casablanca* had been. Costing $3 million, the picture had rentals of $7 million and eight Oscar nominations – its single winner was Katina Paxinou. But opening in the summer of 1943, *For Whom the Bell Tolls* followed *Casablanca* into theatres and seemed to suggest that Ingrid Bergman was the screen's essential wartime heroine (to be followed by Greer Garson as Mrs Miniver). The Oscar for best actress that year gave the early last laugh to David Selznick: it went to Jennifer Jones in *The Song of Bernadette*. History has reordered the vote: the world now assumes that Ingrid won for *Casablanca*.

Almost immediately, as *For Whom the Bell Tolls* ended, Warner Brothers picked up its two stars and put them in *Saratoga Trunk*. They regarded them as 'chemistry', but they were equally prodded by Cooper's wish to stay on a picture with the actress, that heightened state of reality being most conducive to their love affair. While they were up in the mountains for Hemingway, director Sam

Wood had passed the Edna Ferber novel of *Saratoga Trunk* around, and as Ingrid would say, 'We'd had so much fun on *For Whom the Bell Tolls* and got going so well, why shouldn't we make another film together?' The public thought the role of the Creole Clio Dulaine was most suited to Vivien Leigh, but Coop's wishes made the decision. And Selznick simply supervised the paperwork whereby Warners paid him $253,000 for loaning out Ingrid while he paid her her contract due – $69,500. This kind of arithmetic was mounting up on every project. Ingrid and Petter were still very well paid, for Swedes coming to America, but Lindstrom watched the exploitation with increasing indignation.

Saratoga Trunk did not turn out very well, and Gary Cooper would offer the famous rueful remark about he'd never known a girl so much in love as Ingrid until the day the film was over when he couldn't get her on the telephone. As it was, *Saratoga Trunk* was held up a while and released only after the next shooting project – *Gaslight*.

As *Gas Light* (originally), this was a play by Patrick Hamilton that opened in London in December 1938. It concerned a married couple, the Manninghams (played by Gwen Ffrangcon-Davies and Dennis Arundell), where the husband is gradually driving the wife mad. His reason for this is so that he can make a more thorough search of the house where they live so that he can find the jewellery that belonged to a previous owner. That arc of back-story is pretty far-fetched, and does not seem to have interested Hamilton too much. As a bleak connoisseur of marriage and its traps, he was more attentive to the attempt to make a companion believe she is going mad – a process since known as 'gaslighting'.

The play was a hit and it came to New York, opening in 1942 as *Angel Street* (with Judith Evelyn and Vincent Price). Ingrid was one of those who saw the New York production and thrilled to the melodrama as Mrs Manningham feels the gaslight in the house diminishing and believes she hears someone walking in the attic above her. In London and New York, that moment of theatre was key to the success of the productions.

In the meantime, the story was filmed in England, in 1940, as *Gaslight*, directed by Thorold Dickinson, and starring Anton Walbrook and Diana Wynyard. This is a very accomplished film, with rather more emphasis put on Walbrook's malice than on his wife's ordeal. Whereupon, Metro-Goldwyn-Mayer bought up the rights to the play and to the British film. That allowed them to collect and either destroy or lock up every print of the British film so that they would be free to make their own version. That piratical business tactic was shameful, and it provoked a good deal of outrage in the British film industry. Still, that should not get in the way of this judgement: that the British film is a very good melodrama, and the American something of a higher order.

The first idea at Metro was to have Vincente Minnelli

direct, and both Irene Dunne and Hedy Lamarr were talked of in the female role. But then John Van Druten and Walter Reisch began to develop a screenplay. They saw this limitation to Hamilton's original: that it plunges us into the husband's attempt on the wife's sanity, without properly introducing the two characters. So in the rewrite they sketched in a backstory whereby we see Paula Alving as a teenager, traumatized by the unsolved murder of her aunt. She goes to Europe to develop her singing. But the teacher knows her heart isn't in it because she's fallen in love with the humble pianist who works with the teacher, named Gregory Anton. They marry. There is a moment of bliss and then Gregory suggests that they go back to the house in London where Paula once lived, where the murder took place.

These extra scenes are handled very quickly but they make Paula so much more vulnerable: for now we feel that she loves Gregory. So his subtle, almost tender suggestions that she loses things, then hides them, fall on fertile ground. The threat upon her sanity is made real, and it hinges on the same dulcet tone in both their voices. Some actors look good together, but Boyer and Bergman were radio voices stroking each other.

George Cukor was now hired to direct, and David Selznick prevailed upon his father-in-law, Louis B. Mayer, to cast Ingrid as Paula. The screenwriters despaired: 'Ingrid Bergman is a powerful woman,' said Reisch, 'with enormous shoulders, strong, healthy, and no man on earth can talk her into being silly or insane.'

But Cukor was wiser. That's the challenge, he said, and as he thought about Ingrid's fling with Gary Cooper he may have guessed that she was more shaky than she looked. After all, she was an actress! Who ever heard of a strong, secure woman taking that course in life? Who ever heard of so healthy and fearless a woman consenting to the *Gaslight* loan-out deal: $253,000 to Selznick International, and $69,500 to Miss Bergman? The cast was filled out with Charles Boyer (as Gregory) and Joseph Cotten (another Selznick loan-out) as the London police detective who comes to Paula's aid.

Reisch would say later that the whole thing worked because everyone involved had a sense of humour: so Ingrid could play weak and Boyer (the great lover) could turn nasty, while the enormously adept Cukor kept it all under control. There are other assets the film has: first the adapted screenplay and its fuller sense of a story; then there is the exquisite art direction, credited officially to Cedric Gibbons, William Ferrari and Edwin B. Willis, but actually due to Paul Huldschinsky, a German refugee recruited by Cukor – and able to make the claustrophobic house a true character in the film; and finally the use of Joseph Ruttenberg as photographer – the man who had captured Ingrid's sensuality in *Dr Jekyll and Mr Hyde*.

So what works is the germ in Hamilton's story – the idea that love and marital ties may be a cover for incipient madness, and the great effort by Paula to rally her reason and insist on what she knows. Cukor began by

Gaslight

giving Ingrid a context for every set-up, but she told him, 'I'm not a dumb Swede, I know where we are.' Even so, the method worked very well and guided Bergman through a picture where there is a danger of monotony in so many scenes where she feels destabilized. What Ruttenberg showed was the vestige of real illness under her eyes and in her cheeks – it is the story of an increasingly imprisoned woman, and what it begins to discover is a kind of masochism in Ingrid that may want to be tortured. I don't think this would be apparent in *Gaslight* alone, but Bergman's later vein of suffering is opened up here for the first time.

The arc of the film ends in the moment when Paula has Gregory tied up in a chair, and then she taunts him by pretending that he might be going mad. The vengeance is both earned and earnest, and a very gratifying end to the melodrama. But it is most interesting in showing us an actress who begins to be powerful (or not) because of her accomplishments. Will Paula be 'well' again at the end of the story? Or has she laid down the rails for an emotional switchback in her own soul? Will she feel compelled to go on the stage?

Gaslight was a big hit, nominated for seven Oscars (though not for Cukor's direction). Boyer was nominated, as was Angela Lansbury, in her debut, as the saucy housemaid. The winners were the quartet for art direction and Ingrid Bergman as best actress – she overcame Claudette Colbert in *Since You Went Away*, Bette Davis in *Mr Skeffington*, Greer Garson in *Mrs Parkington* and Barbara Stanwyck in *Double Indemnity*. That Oscar was the vindication of her decision to go to America, but her family life was increasingly troubled. And for all those who had taken it for granted that Ingrid in person was a tower of strength and courage – as she maintained – *Gaslight* had detected fissures of ordeal and anxiety that might be permanent.

Would playing a nun expose the cracks? In many ways, *The Bells of St Mary's* was the most trivial and least necessary film Ingrid had made in America. If rentals of $8 million are ever trivial or beside the point. It meant – if you overlooked *Saratoga Trunk* – that Ingrid had made five huge hits in a row at a time when movie-going was truly a patriotic pursuit. And now, as well as being heroic, adorable and lovely, she had taken upon herself the nun's costume. When the storm clouds opened on Ingrid, nothing inspired them more than the daft, pious memory of her Sister Benedict. That was the last straw in betrayal, and the touchpaper for the kindling at her stake.

The Bells of St Mary's was a shameless sequel to *Going My Way*, the Best Picture of 1943 (it defeated *Double Indemnity*!), in which Leo McCarey almost single-handedly created the genre of parochial comedy. It was a battle of generations as easy-going Father O'Malley (Bing Crosby) attempted to reform the old-school methods of Father Fitzgibbon (Barry Fitzgerald) at a Catholic school for boys. (Both Crosby and Fitzgerald won Oscars.) O'Malley is a songwriter, too, and the songs raise money for the Church. So there were children, and songs, and animals, plus the immense cunning of Mr McCarey himself, a great director of comedy and a cheerful purveyor of sweet homilies to fit your worst dreams. The whole thing is a calculated yet wide-eyed disgrace, with rentals of $6.5 million. It had all been cooked up at RKO, and it would have been a miracle if that studio had overcome the prayers of so many millions and stopped the sequel.

So McCarey reckoned to play the old game again. This time it was at a school where O'Malley's 'modernism' was at odds with the by-the-book approach of Sister Benedict, a nun from Sweden originally (Ingrid actually sings a song in Swedish) and she has been three times in a row Best Face in a Wimple. No, I made that up. But employing a costume that concentrated on just her face did wonders for Ingrid's beauty. She liked the robes a lot, she said, because they allowed her to indulge her greatest weakness – snacking. Weight problems were already affecting her career, but in those robes everyone is thin.

What else? Well, the school needs a new building, and there's a question as to whether the local skinflint (Henry Travers) will donate it to the Church or not. Then there's Sister's getting a little touch of TB, O'Malley's weird resemblance to Bing Crosby – 'You have a dishonest face', Benedict tells him off at one point, and it's a remark we can't forget or argue away. McCarey had a knack for doing these things with so many positive touches that you begin to forgive the crushing horrors. The kids improvise. The animals are cute. O'Malley is so restful you could fall asleep. And Ingrid's final close-up comes very close to a sudden beatification: out of the sludge of sentimentality an instant arises of authentic spiritual radiance. No, of course, she shouldn't have done the film, but there are moments when she is so noble or hopeful it takes your breath away.

But then consider the deal that allowed Ingrid to be Sister Benedict. Selznick had been opposed to letting Ingrid do the film – he said he thought sequels were vulgar and almost bound to be disappointing. But Leo McCarey prayed and persevered, and this is how it came down: Selznick received $175,000 in cash; he got the free use of Gregory Peck for a film that would be *Spellbound*; he was given the remake rights for *Little Women*; and he was granted free use of studio facilities at RKO. That package was said to be worth about $450,000. In return, Ingrid got nearly $100,000. Some people marvelled that McCarey had accepted such tough terms – but then the picture opened and $8 million in rentals swam into sight.

The parochial comedy had its moment in the 1930s and '40s. Spencer Tracy had sometimes been the priest challenging the rascal Clark Gable. Pat O'Brien played the same role with Cagney. But the idea of a comedy about the affairs of a small parish really derives from McCarey's two films at the end of the war. It would take a brave rationalist to assert that the two films are not close to the notion of a Roman Catholic America fit to save the world, and yet no film critic ever made the claim that the separation of Church and State was enough to condemn the films as U for Unconstitutional. The other miracle is that there were not more attempts to cash in on this example. Where did that much good taste come from in this land where Bing Crosby croons the Latin lyrics to many an old song?

As for Ingrid, it's easy to argue that *The Bells of St Mary's* was a lark for her. There is a nice story how, at the very end of the film, she had the assembled cast and crew laughing by suddenly kissing O'Malley full on his startled lips as she leaves for the dry air of Arizona. It is said that Crosby was not amused – but Bing and Ingrid did not gel, except in the soft-shoe shuffle of McCarey's dialogue. She felt that Bing was always surrounded by yes-men. Did she believe in the film – for a moment? It's a fair question when one recalls that in 1948 a man named Roberto Rossellini made a film, *L'Amore*, which includes an episode, 'Il Miracolo', in which a crazy peasant woman, having been seduced by a scoundrel believes she has been impregnated by Christ.

One last aside on this matter: in *The Godfather*, at Christmas time, Michael and Kay come out of a screening of *The Bells of St Mary's*. It is hard to read their reaction, and Francis Coppola may not have meant to make McCarey's film any part of his. But immediately Michael sees a newspaper headline reporting that his father has been gunned down. At this point, Michael is the Ivy League kid, still, a nice clean boy, the war hero, who has been kept out of the family business. Then in the next passage of the film, he becomes not just his father's bodyguard and avenger, but the strictest member of the Corleone family. It's going too far – I am provoked by its sweeping invasive spoliage on matters of intelligence – but *The Bells of St Mary's* is the breakfast of tyranny.

If you've been keeping count, David O. Selznick has so far received money or the equivalent close to $1 million, while he has paid his golden client, Ingrid Bergman, his natural actress, a little over $200,000. In addition, he had gone a little crazy, when that was a fashionable Hollywood condition and not just the way of the world. David Selznick had always tried very hard to be the best. His father had gone broke in the picture business. David's older brother, Myron, had always told the kid he was a chump and an idiot. And then, in supreme self-vindication, the chump had carried off Best Picture two years in a row – with *Gone With the Wind* and *Rebecca* – and made a fortune. What next?

The immature persona cracked without a goal like that of *Gone With the Wind*. He was exhausted, and he believed he needed a great rest. That took many forms – gambling, in which his consistency as a loser amazed every hardened veteran taught to believe that the odds moved back and forth; behaving like an agent, to rival his brother Myron, who always teased and

intimidated the kid brother, but who was by then a fal-
tering alcoholic; dreaming of being involved in the
war – when any nation would have seen the wisdom of
keeping Selznick as far from military operation or thinking as possible; and generally leading a life outside the
confines of his marriage. Irene had been a 'perfect' wife
in that she was as born for the business as David could
ever claim. But warmth was not her long suit, and
actresses (or messenger girls) can do warmth and sincerity at the drop of ... well, easily. So David O. Selznick
began to behave so badly that his wife – who cared
mightily for the family fortune – came to believe that he
was having a breakdown.

That was a measure of her insight and of the way she
might have been a doctor. But, other people asked, what
does David O. Selznick have to be depressed about
when he has everything? Perhaps the everything is the
trouble, she surmised, for Irene Selznick was one of the
generation that had learned psychology and scorned
Hollywood wealth. It is a complex history, but in the
1930s – because of all manner of persecution in Europe – many highly educated people, some of them
Jewish, had come to America and to Los Angeles. And
they had Freud in their luggage. There were even some
analysts and practitioners trained in Vienna and startled
to find how fertile the fields of make-believe were for
their new way of explaining human behaviour. After all,
if Ilsa Lund can't decide between Rick or Victor, then
maybe the actress playing her part would be interested

to hear a professional estimate of Ilsa's uncertainty. In their own way, actors had been on to the usefulness of sense memory and character analysis for some time – at least since the onset of the close-up and its implication, that an inner life existed.

Irene Selznick took advice and heard of a woman – Dr May Romm – benign, intelligent, exceptional and in Los Angeles. She coaxed David into a few sessions. He was a reprobate. He turned up hours too late at times that suited him – he carried his childishness before him like a flag. But May Romm was intrigued and patient and just a little star-struck perhaps. She waited out her client's infantile delays, and soon enough she engaged his interest. After a few sessions, David Selznick summed up the process as follows – it was a medium he knew already from story conferences where you sat around mulling over a character and their motivation. But now, said the producer, all the talk was about him. About me! That charmed him. So he plunged into 'therapy', felt better in half an hour and – in his own considerable, if inept, kindness – insisted that Dr May Romm have a credit as technical adviser on a film to be called *Spellbound*, a picture that would explain psycho-analysis to the general public.

It's easy to make fun of, but in truth the intellectual climate of the time was very drawn to analysis. In previous wars it had been enough to say some men were brave and others were not, but it was during the Second World War that nervous stress, battle fatigue and tor-

ture became respectable subjects. As war ended, everyone was asking simple but profound questions about
where Nazi evil had come from and how factories of
destruction – Auschwitz or Hiroshima – could be coun-
tenanced. Human behaviourism was a more open, tol-
erant field. Mental breakdown was not mere weakness,
or self-indulgence. The Selznicks became devotees of
analysis and many in the extended family had a spell on
the couch. Quite literally, David believed it was a subject for a movie. And, as if to prove that he was a
reformed (or restrained) character, he decided to hire
directly two of the properties he owned but had been
loaning out – Alfred Hitchcock and Ingrid Bergman.

Those two people had joined Selznick International at
about the same time (and they do show that the chump
in Selznick had a special instinct for talent). They must
have met during the early 1940s at Selznick parties. But it
was *Spellbound* that forged the bond, and established a
strange kind of love affair. By then, 1945, it was common
enough knowledge inside Hollywood that the sweet, sincere Ingrid was promiscuous and oddly unattached to
her family. It was also becoming clear that Hitchcock – a
dry, funny man, but famously unattractive – formed
intense attachments to beautiful actresses that might
stay as fantasy and might break out in real, awkward
incidents. I don't think it's too much to say that in seeing Ingrid, Hitch took extra flight as an artist and a man.
Observers on *Spellbound* noticed that he flirted with
Ingrid all the time and told her dirty jokes, remarking

on her body. For her part, the actress giggled and told him not to be a naughty boy. To this day, we don't know how much farther it went. But actresses had much to gain; Hitch invariably made their best pictures.

Spellbound is a very silly movie, but one that dazzled in 1945. We are at a large rural mental institution from which one director, Dr Murchison (Leo G. Carroll), has just resigned. The staff, including the earnest and bespectacled Dr Constance Petersen (Bergman) awaits the new director – who proves to be Dr Edwardes (Gregory Peck). In 1945, Peck was 29, while Ingrid was 30. This leaves one under the impression that preferment comes early in the young science of American analysis. Alas, the entire process of scrutiny seems to be a lot slacker: Peck is not just a beautiful kid, he rather suspects he is a murderer. We doubt this (for we know stardom), but still he does seem more suited to being a patient in his own hospital than its leader.

In the end, order is sorted out, the real murderer is punished and the ship of psychiatry can sail on serenely. There is a famous dream sequence – by Salvador Dalí – and there are several ravishing cinematic effects where Hitch (a psycho-minded fellow, if ever there was one) shows off his own expression of the inner life through camera style. Constance rescues Dr Edwardes and she is a woman of great pluck and ingenuity, as well as the measure of suspense – the posters for the film asked the question, 'Will he kiss her or will he kill her?' A later Hitchcock might have left us more uncertain and uneasy

about Edwardes (and Peck is so beautiful he could hide
an angel of death). But in this film, we have to recog-
nize the limitation that Pauline Kael complained about:
'It was fitting, of course, that the actress who was once
described as a "fine, strong, cow-country maiden" should
be cast as a good solid, competent analyst, dispensing
cures and murder solutions with the wholesome sim-
plicity of a mother adding wheatgerm to the family diet,
but Bergman's famous "sincerity", has rarely been so
out of place as in this confection whipped up by jaded
chefs.'

But now turn to the facts of what happened. *Spellbound* did nearly $5 million in rentals, and it was nomi-
nated for Best Picture, photography and score (where it
won). Ingrid was not nominated, but only because her
sincerity in *The Bells of St Mary's* was apparently more
persuasive – was America still readier to settle for a nun
than a good doctor? Plainly nothing in the cockamamie
narrative of *Spellbound* had dislodged Ingrid Bergman
as the essential heroine of the post-war moment. It is
easier to see now that *Spellbound* was just as hokey or
foolish as *Casablanca* and *Gaslight* were precisely effec-
tive. But for the moment, Ingrid was a coverlet and a
comforter to draw up in any crisis, as well as the surest
thing the box office knew.

Something else entered Ingrid's life as the war ended.
Like many glamorous stars, she began to undertake
trips and tours to entertain the troops. She believed her

privilege had earned this duty and she exulted in it. And it helped restore the part of her that was 'European', and not just the mysterious European woman in immense fantasies about America and the rest of the world. She wanted to believe she was down-to-earth, 'sincere', and appreciative of real heroics. Like Marlene Dietrich – who was moved in very much the same way – Ingrid was as struck by ordinary soldiers as by officers. She kissed them all and she travelled and toured in war-torn Europe and began to realize what real war was like. There's little doubt but that this underlined her own sense of herself as a figure representing the Europe of refugees.

A key step in this growth occurred in June 1945. Ingrid was on an entertainment tour, with Jack Benny, Martha Tilton and Larry Adler (and she was having an affair with the harmonica virtuoso). In Paris, staying at the Ritz, she was invited out by two buddies on the prowl – the writer Irwin Shaw and the photographer Robert Capa. Not without reason (for he had a fierce gypsy charm as well as the scent of danger), she fell madly in love with Capa. And he was the real thing: he had staggered ashore on D-Day taking photographs; he had been in Robert Jordan's Spain and taken that momentous picture of the death of a partisan – even if that photograph was just a touch rigged. He was Hungarian, a womanizer, a danger-hound and a real man. He took her to see the damaged Europe, the one not on the official tours. He took her to Berlin. He photographed her in a bath tossed out on the street. She would kiss any soldier she saw for Capa's lens. And the excitement was so intense I think it changed her life and reminded her of 'reality'. Ahead lay a great change – a mad sideways move, if you like – and I don't think it would have happened but for Capa and the way he re-educated her. If you want to think about it more deeply, just imagine a conversation in Berlin in 1945 where he tells her what he thinks of *The Bells of St Mary's* and she realizes that America is not the whole world, not for someone who was once half German.

Ingrid took these trips despite Petter's requests that she spend more time with him and their daughter, Pia. Ingrid often talked about the hardship and sorrow of being separated from her family, but as Petter saw it she did not do too much to alter the balance. She accepted every invitation to work or travel. She seemed possessed. I suspect she felt she had a special vocation and responsibility and that she leaned towards the things she did well. Don't we all do the same? Still, the pressure was building.

For the first time in her American life, in *Notorious*, Ingrid played a woman who was German. It was a Hitchcock dream, to have Ingrid in a film about espionage, but with a very personal twist: 'I wanted to make this film about a man who forces a woman to go to bed with another man because it's his professional duty.' Ben Hecht came on board as the writer (he had done *Spellbound*, too) and they both thought of a South American setting. In the months just after the close of the European war, there were stories of Nazis who had gone into hiding in South American dictatorships where no questions were asked.

So Alicia Huberman (Bergman) is the daughter of a man who has been executed as a Nazi spy. She is taken up by T. R. Devlin (Cary Grant), an unusually detached, if not chilly, American security agent. Alicia has crashed since her father's death: she is an alcoholic, promiscuous and depressed to a suicidal point. But Devlin wants to use her – he is so instructed – to uncover the rest of her father's spy ring. So he pretends to fall in love with her, only to find that acting is the short step to believing. And so he has to instruct the woman he loves to meet the mysterious Alexander Sebastian (Claude Rains) who lives in Rio with his mother. Sebastian is a Nazi spy but he's a man with real feelings, too, and he falls in love with Alicia. Marry him, says Devlin. She takes the challenge, just as Ingrid was always ready for self-abuse. But Sebastian discovers the truth and begins a slow process of poisoning his wife. Can Devlin rescue her?

It is a love story for sadomasochists; indeed, it is far more intriguingly about psychology than *Spellbound*. At first, it was a picture that Selznick intended to produce himself, as a way of cashing in on the success of *Spellbound*. Hitchcock was not happy about that proximity. Ever since their fights over *Rebecca*, Hitch had judged it far better to be loaned out by Selznick than working for him directly. Fate came to the aid of the English director.

With Grant in *Notorious*

Selznick left his wife in 1945 and bit the bullet of Jennifer Jones. He was determined to display her stardom and her sexiness in a Western, *Duel in the Sun*, and to make that picture into a success that would outstrip *Gone With the Wind*.

Duel in the Sun had location work in Arizona, and it had problems directly congruent with Selznick's urge to interfere. In the end, the mogul went so far as to form his own distribution company, solely for the purpose of releasing that one film. His judgement was shot, but *Notorious* was the beneficiary. Selznick made a deal with RKO whereby he packaged *Notorious*, its cast and crew and sold it off to the smaller studio with the proviso that he would retain 50 per cent of its profits.

The most important thing to say about *Notorious* is that it marks an adult intensification in Hitchcock's work. In great part, that comes from the sadomasochistic balance of the story and the way Ingrid Bergman can inhabit that feeling. Alicia is a fallen woman in search of redemption, but along the way she will become virtually a whore who comes close to losing all faith in love. And if the downside is steep and grim, then the love is headier. *Notorious* has the first extended kiss sequence from Hitchcock. There were written or unwritten laws in the Code that a screen kiss could last only a few seconds. After that, it ran the risk of being foreplay. So Hitch deliberately broke a kiss down into many smaller kisses. Cary Grant was able to do this, and Ingrid Bergman was able to respond to it. And so the kiss seems like the prelude to sex, and the suspense element of the story is one on which real lives depend.

After that, of course, Alicia Huberman is another version of Paula Alving, a woman going mad or sinking towards her doom in the stricken belief that she deserves this fate. So Alicia is not just poisoned, she is deeply demoralized, like a broken religious spirit. It follows that what Hitchcock revealed here was Ingrid's readiness to be an everywoman figure in some bottomless parable about good and evil. That makes *Notorious* the sort of film Roberto Rossellini might have seen and learned from – if he was that kind of movie director.

There are things in *Notorious* that are just fun – like the chance use of uranium as the plot MacGuffin when that element was actually a real player in the drama of America's secret nuclear practice. But the way in which Alicia is experimented with is not playful at all. You can say that Hitchcock's employment of espionage was abstract and providential – he just wanted something that would put Alicia and the audience through an ordeal. But the ordeal is not simply physical. It represents a culture that no longer takes life very seriously. Cruelty has crept into being a norm. And when Devlin goes back to rescue her, and guides her down the perilous staircase in Sebastian's house, it is all of life that is being defended, and Bergman's dark-eyed exhaustion speaks to it. Just as she had in *Gaslight*, Ingrid could make her sanity seem like a test for the world. Courage, courage! But realize that the world thinks it owns you, or has invented you.

Notorious concluded Ingrid's contract with David Selznick. And now the two parties looked at each other in wary dismay. Selznick had discovered her at a time when probably no other Hollywood organization would have gone to Sweden to persuade her. The Selznicks had looked after her personally and they thought they were her friends. David personally had taught her so much and won for her several key roles that established her status and allowed her to flower as an actress. They had made her and her family rich.

All of these things, and many more, were expressed by David in one of his special memos – it was a description of their contract years, as if written by Ingrid to Selznick. The concept is funny enough for a bit, but then it becomes ponderous, a sign of Selznick's terrible imperial view of himself. What the letter omits is how remorselessly Selznick had milked Ingrid and profited from her. Was that illegal? No. Was it a little tasteless? Yes – and it put an extra strain on the impossible marriage with Petter, for Ingrid did not care to fight those business battles herself. She relied on Petter, a good dentist who turned himself into a passable agent and who became a very unwelcome figure at Selznick parties.

It was Petter who pushed the claim that, while Ingrid had entertained the troops, she had missed her last picture commitment to Selznick – it might have been *The Spiral Staircase, The Farmer's Daughter* or *To Each His Own* – so that Selznick now owed her a final $60,000.

That was a tough point to make and it left Selznick feeling wounded and slighted. In the peroration of 'her' letter to him, therefore, he had her say this:

Throughout the years, you devoted an enormous amount of time to going over material for me, and to reading scripts submitted from every studio in town, in order to be sure that I was the first actress in the history of the screen that had her pick of the best stories of every studio in town, plus the insistence of yourself as to how the picture should be set up and who should make them in each department. This insistence on your part meant that I had Fleming, Cukor, Curtiz, Wood, McCarey as my directors; that I had the best cameramen in the business, all selected and approved by you, since I didn't know any of them; that I had Spencer Tracy, Gary Cooper, Charles Boyer, Joseph Cotten, Bing Crosby, Gregory Peck, Cary Grant as my leading men . . .

When everyone else in Hollywood disbelieved in me and wondered why you had brought me over, and through the long period when you couldn't lend me to anyone, and through the secondary period when you were loaning me at cost and at less than cost, you insisted that I was the great actress of this generation, that I would be the greatest star in the industry, that I would be the Academy Award winner, that I would be universally acclaimed.

A woman might run to escape memos like that. Still, I think any objective observer pities both of them at the moment of parting: they liked each other, and they needed each other. I have suggested earlier that a prolonged personal relationship with Ingrid might have steadied Selznick. The possibility works the other way round. As it was, the friendship never cut out altogether. After David was with Jennifer, and when Ingrid needed advice, she talked to Irene Selznick – one of her lasting friends.

She had been friendly with the novelist Erich Maria Remarque, and so she agreed to appear in the film of his *Arch of Triumph*, a very moody study of refugees in Paris in 1938. It was made for Enterprise Productions. David Lewis produced and Lewis Milestone directed, and Harry Brown wrote the script after Irwin Shaw had failed at the task. There's enough left to see why the several parties thought it might be an important film. There's a heartfelt performance from Charles Boyer, a lurid one from Charles Laughton (as the Nazi menace), panache from Louis Calhern and endless, sultry close-ups of Ingrid's glorious gloom surrounded by shadow. But as she knew at the time, the picture was a muddle. When it turned out far too long it was cut to pieces and wreckage was left. It had ended up costing $4 million. Ingrid's contract had given her 25 per cent of the profits – but there were none. At long last, in America, she had made a serious failure. Selznick must have sighed.

*   *   *

Arch of Triumph opened in March 1948. It was at some time not long thereafter, in New York, that Ingrid, with Petter, saw the movie, *Paisan*, by Roberto Rossellini. Shortly thereafter, she said, no it was *Open City*, his earlier film. But we know she saw *Open City* in 1946, in the company of a young publicist, Joseph Steele, hired by Selznick to look after Ingrid, but inclined to take that task all too personally. They had been impressed with *Open City*, but nothing had happened. And now Ingrid saw another Rossellini picture – a good deal less vivid than *Open City*, but utterly committed to telling the real story of Italy at the end of the war. She decided to be amazed and altered by it.

I put it that way because, as she neared 35, Ingrid Bergman was worried about her career. Under Selznick she had been able to take shelter, and to enjoy their luck together. No one had had such luck. But now Ingrid was on her own in a changed world: by 1948, it was becoming clear that Hollywood's old authority was diminished. Public tastes had changed. Television was coming. The studios had lost a court decision and were now obliged to sell off their theatres. Costs had risen very fast. Who could have predicted that *Arch of Triumph* was headed for disaster with Boyer and Bergman? Ingrid was thinking of other things: of doing Joan of Arc on stage and film; and she had another commitment to Hitchcock that would be *Under Capricorn*. But she needed more.

She asked Irene Selznick what to do, and it seems

likely that it was Irene's suggestion that she at least send a letter to Rossellini. No one in America knew too much about him, beyond the fact that he was a director and seemed to be personally involved with Anna Magnani, the actress in his *Open City*. But together they found an address that might work, and Ingrid sent this message, a letter, that said, 'If you need a Swedish actress who in Italian knows only "ti amo" I am ready to come and make a film with you.'

In 1948, Roberto Rossellini was 42 years old. As a kid, he had been obsessed with cinema and its instruments and in the late 1930s he accepted an invitation from the Fascists (and from Mussolini's son) to help on a picture about flying. He pursued that work for a few years until the breakdown of the Fascist government. It was then, with very limited resources and in real danger, that he directed *Open City* – a study of Rome as the Nazis still controlled it and the city awaited the Allies. *Open City* was a sensation all over the world when it showed, and it was regarded as a pioneering work of Italian neo-realism. That was followed by *Paisan*, *Germany Year Zero* (about an orphan struggling to survive in the ruined Berlin), and *L'Amore*, a vehicle for Rossellini's mistress, Anna Magnani. He had married Marcella De Marchis in 1936, and they had two children, Romano, who had died in 1946 at the age of 9, and Renzo, born in 1941. Rossellini was close to exhausted from the harsh conditions and meagre reward of neo-realism. He was a man who liked dining out with glamorous women, and who collected sports cars. He was an Italian director who was bursting with the possibility of going to America to make an authentically commercial picture! So what did he do when he got the letter? He cabled back to say how touched he was and he told the actress that he had been dreaming of a film for her. What would you have said?

Later on, when her letter became public, gossips surmised over the 'ti amo'. But I think that was literally about all Ingrid knew in Italian: it was actually a phrase that had figured in *Arch of Triumph*. Indeed, when it came to love, Ingrid had a much bigger affair to be done with before she could turn to Rossellini.

In every dispute with Selznick, Ingrid could point to the way she had been 'denied' her Joan of Arc. And at the time of *Intermezzo*, she had been the age of the real maid at her death. Apparently, she never lost her admiration for the historical figure or the way in which Joan represented the untapped part of the actress. The playwright Maxwell Anderson heard the cry and delivered a play, *Joan of Lorraine*, in which an acting company discuss their production of the play and try to make Joan a 'modern' character. In real life, the play met a problem not taken up in these discussions. On the road, in Washington DC, Ingrid discovered that she was expected to play in a segregated theatre and she refused.

The play opened on Broadway in 1946. The reviews were poor, but most critics responded to Ingrid's sincerity

in what was a tedious play. And so it became a hit –
and so, in turn, people talked of doing it as a movie.
Ingrid won prizes. She earned about $130,000. And
she enjoyed living in a New York hotel, with most of
her lovers at hand. And then one day, a new one
appeared. Victor Fleming – the man who had directed
Ingrid in *Dr Jekyll and Mr Hyde* – came backstage after
a performance. Fleming was 62, alcoholic and with a
heart condition. He had made only three pictures since
Jekyll and Hyde and he was desperate for a hit that might
match the moment in which he'd signed off on *Gone
With the Wind* and *The Wizard of Oz*. In fact, he had
another project in mind the night he came to see *Joan
of Lorraine*, but in the theatre he was so moved by
Ingrid that he knew there was no other project to
match it.

And so began perhaps the saddest venture of Ingrid's
career: the movie of *Joan of Arc*, made as Ingrid and
Fleming conducted a gloomy affair, for the director was
certain he was dying. Walter Wanger came on board as
producer. Anderson and Andrew Solt turned the play
into a film script, junking the entire apparatus of the
theatre company debating the play and settling for a
vague, fifteenth-century approach – the characters wear
period costume, there are castles and battles, and yet
the whole thing has a distilled look and a seeming
economy with crowds so that it comes as a surprise
to discover that the picture was allowed to cost over
$4.5 million.

Fleming yielded to Ingrid on most things, above all on her wish to drop Anderson's concept for her own. A string of secondary writers were brought in, and Ingrid was pretty ruthless about imposing her will on her weakened lover. Indeed, she was possessed, hearing her own voices and little else:

I get so angry when I read Fleming's letters. He seems to have to spend day after day with business people; everyone trying to find out where and how to get the last dollar out of the picture. I know Victor has talked business much more than story, but it is important I guess to get these things organized after all. He said last time we spoke on the phone, that now he is only concentrating on story . . . I'll be the bridge for everyone who wants to come to Victor with ideas. Don't think for a moment I believe I can turn Victor round my little finger, but I'll try to talk like an angel, be strong like a god, and dangerous like a devil. Forward my friends. Now starts the battle for Joan!

The shooting did not prosper. Joan seems too old and too sophisticated, and when she appears in shining aluminum armour the tone of animated films or kids' heroics is unhappily close. Fleming himself knew it was a disaster, without ever quite understanding why. He showed the film to his old friend, John Lee Mahin, and asked him, why, why, it had turned out so badly. Mahin replied, 'Vic, it's the first film she's directed.'

It opened in New York in November 1948 to killing

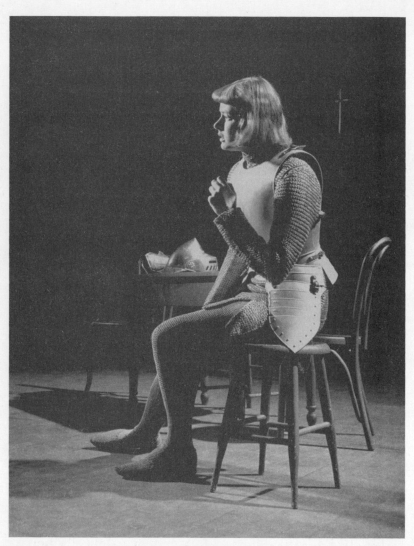

Joan of Arc

reviews. In the event, the public remained intrigued, and the film did modestly well at the box office. But Fleming was the casualty: he died in January 1949.

By a generous account, Ingrid Bergman's life was in chaos. She was with Petter still, yet she had been entertaining thoughts of going off with Larry Adler or Robert Capa (two devastating lone wolves) – if either one really offered a settled state – and she had had her tragic romance with Victor Fleming. All the while, Roberto Rossellini was the mystery card – as yet unmet – but assuring her by letter that he had plans, dreams and more. And it was in that crazed moment that she made *Under Capricorn* for Alfred Hitchcock.

In their unique ways, it is likely that Rossellini, Fleming and Hitchcock all loved her – whether they had met her or not, people fell for Ingrid. But I wonder if any director had a deeper understanding of her than Hitchcock. If she had only made *Under Capricorn*, she would be a phenomenon – or a cult.

Hitchcock had nursed the material, a 1937 novel by Helen Simpson, for some time. He said he was waiting on Ingrid being ready, and he always spoke of it as her project, or as a story intended to showcase her. It is set in Australia in 1831, and it concerns an ill-assorted couple, the Fluskys. She is an aristocrat married to a former groom, but she is an alcoholic wreck because she has allowed her husband to cover up a crime she committed. The insight here is that of *Notorious*, that something in the noble Ingrid craved being degraded, or brought close to ruin – anything that would require a long, painful moral rehabilitation. For some time before filming could begin, Hitchcock and Hume Cronyn had been working on a screenplay for a production Hitch intended as an independent venture. He would form a company with his London friend Sydney Bernstein and the film would be shot in Britain.

On his previous venture, *Rope*, Hitchcock had departed from his normal, fragmented style to shoot in 'ten-minute takes'. As if aping the fluid, tracking scrutiny of, say, Renoir, Mizoguchi or Ophuls, Hitch set up elaborate full-magazine shots and timed his unavoidable cuts for moments of darkness when they would not be seen. It was an abstract experiment, at odds with nearly every instinct in Hitchcock. On *Under Capricorn*, he was in a transitional state, abandoning the arbitrary task of keeping the camera running, but still using some very long, intricate shots to mount a searching study of Bergman's desire to escape.

Ingrid did not appreciate this way of working, where hours or days might be spent on the mechanics of a complicated shot, while she got to deliver maybe only every other day. She was Hollywood-trained by now: she knew the pattern of master shot and close-ups, the sensible, industrial way of putting pictures together, and though she admired Hitch and often trusted him, she was terribly frustrated. It was then that she ate too much, and drank. She looks tragically beautiful in *Under*

Capricorn but she knew how much care needed to be taken now.

The script is interesting now, we've got a pretty good end, but Hitch's new technique I don't like. I have had no experience with it yet, for my first entrance was just a normal shot. But I have watched him with the others. It is so frightening for actors and crew. If the least bit goes wrong, you know . . . I think Hitch and I will have some arguments. He wanted to shoot a whole roll of film, the camera following me everywhere and the sets and furniture being pulled away. It meant we had to rehearse a whole day without shooting and then shoot the scenes the following day. It made everybody nervous, but he insisted. We already had one little argument about my entrance and I got my way. I know I can always win with him, but I dislike the argument.

It got worse. There were days when the unthinkable occurred. There was a dispute and Hitchcock left his own set in silence. Of course, very quickly – by his next film, *Stage Fright* – Hitch had given up this elaborate scheme of shooting and he never really went back to it. Still, the passage just quoted speaks to the underground feelings between the two of them: his adoration, and his weakness because of it. Many accounts of Hitch and actresses paint him as the bully, but his love was often close to awe and shyness. When Ingrid altered her whole life for another director, Hitchcock was shocked and wounded. The two of them never came close to working together again, and yet I think Hitchcock believed he had found his perfect actress. Suppose things had worked out differently, Ingrid might have had the lead roles in *Dial M for Murder*, *Rear Window* and even *Vertigo*. That is not to belittle Grace Kelly or Kim Novak, both of whom brought youth on their side. But Ingrid would have been only 42 in *Vertigo* – and I think she could have done the haunted sisterhood of Madeleine Elster and Judy Barton.

If you want the proof, look at *Under Capricorn*. It is a good story: the marriage and the social uplift that have been built on the servant taking the blame for the mistress's crime; the damage done to love because of it; and the feeling of civilization on the edge of the desert. *Under Capricorn* is assisted by one fine performance from Joseph Cotten – red-headed, gruff, aggrieved – and another from Margaret Leighton as an antipodean Mrs Danvers. What it cannot overcome is the spry inadequacy of Michael Wilding in the other lead part – yet *Dial M for Murder* manages to make us forget Robert Cummings. There is no forgetting Ingrid's unwinding confessional speech where she keeps trying to turn away from the camera that will not give up on her. In theory and history, we have to believe in 1948 that Ingrid Bergman was ready to give up on the artifice of studio film-making. Yet she had never been better.

It was during the shooting of *Under Capricorn*, in September 1948, that Ingrid and Roberto Rossellini actually met

With Hitchcock

for the first time. He was in Amalfi, working on a picture.
Anna Magnani was with him, and she was watching him.
Rossellini had told the hotel staff that if any cables came
for him from England they were to be delivered secretly.
At lunch next day, the head waiter slipped the director a
cable. Magnani was mixing the pasta and the sauce, but
she saw the bit of paper and the studious way in which
Rossellini declined to read it.

'So, how is it?' she asked her lover, indicating the
mixed pasta.

He told her it was terrific and she tossed the mix in
his face.

So it was that Rossellini travelled to Paris to meet
Ingrid and Petter at the Hotel George V. It was a friendly
enough meeting, even with Petter trying to enforce a
strict contract, but there were warning signs everywhere.
Roberto had the germ of an idea for what would
become *Stromboli* – a woman refugee goes to live with
an Italian fisherman on the bleak, volcanic island.

She asked how long this film would take. Oh, three
or four weeks, he guessed. So quickly? she marvelled.
And he tried to please her. He said they could take
longer if she wanted. She thought it was the funniest
answer.

What language do we work in? she asked. He thought
and he suggested Swedish. But that's silly, she said. Oh,
well, Italian, if you like, but it doesn't matter because it
will be dubbed anyway.

My clothes? she wondered. Who will design them?

And he told her – she should have listened – your character is very poor. We will simply buy the cheapest clothes at an ordinary shop.

Petter sighed. So Ingrid took him into the next room and said, 'I beg you, don't make the deal too hard on him because I want to work with him. I so love to hear this man, he's so different from anybody else. Don't make the deal hard and difficult because who cares? What I want is just to go to Italy to make this movie. Don't make me lose this picture.'

And so Petter Lindstrom consented and made the feeble arrangements, pretty much ensuring his own grim role in history. He was trapped, I suppose, but trapped by love as much as anything else. Ingrid Bergman was on her way to Stromboli, and it is just a whim of history that imagines this filmography for her instead of the years with Rossellini: *Miss Julie* (Alf Sjöberg); *A Streetcar Named Desire* (Elia Kazan); *Sawdust and Tinsel* (Ingmar Bergman); *Lola Montes* (Max Ophuls); *Vertigo* (Alfred Hitchcock).

This is still a difficult story to tell. A terrible international scandal descended on the couple, shaming to all the ideals and models of behaviour that were invoked. It is true that huge forces of reaction and disapproval were hurled at Ingrid and Roberto, but they were enforced by developments in the international press that had not been realized until that moment. Anyone looking back on what happened feels the hypocrisy of

the outrage, but don't forget the engine of media exul-
tation – this scandal was the first of many, and the first
post-war signal of the rancour and madness caught up
in celebrity. But the frenzy of the campaigns made the
principals afraid to speak out and that adds to the confusion over what really happened. Ingrid and Roberto
gave up existing spouses to marry and to have children
of their own. These are facts – but would those facts
have occurred in the same way if no one had bothered
to notice their affair? So they made a series of films
together when they might have settled for one or two.
There was so much face to be saved and so many awkward human truths that got flattened out – this Ingrid
and Roberto were both reckless opportunists. But they
dived into playing the roles of victims and martyrs. Take
your pick, but allow that neither role was an exact fit.

Nor should we overlook the appealing sidebar of
Anna Magnani, last seen giving a treacherous man all
the pasta at once. *Stromboli* is the more ironic an epic if
one realizes that the first actress Rossellini had talked to
about the idea was Magnani. So, spurned, she began her
own version of the story – *Volcano*. It is not a very good
film, but just as Ingrid had come to Italy so Magnani
would go to Hollywood, winning an Oscar in *The Rose
Tattoo* and playing opposite Burt Lancaster. That was
her way of telling the world that a large part of Roberto
had simply dreamed of living in Beverly Hills – but how
could he manage that once he and Ingrid were known
as 'outlaws'?

How did Roberto sell Ingrid on *Stromboli*? Perhaps it was the idea of going to its remote island where the ground shook? Perhaps it was drama taking over life. Afterwards, when he was talking to film critics – and Roberto cultivated that audience – he was always saying that the woman in the film, a Lithuanian picked out of a refugee camp, was a model of post-war cynicism and alienation, ready for the ordeal that led to spiritual renewal. Did he tell Ingrid that? Did they have enough of any language for that to be conveyed? Or was it quite simply that she was going to be Ingrid Bergman on Stromboli, like Joan at the stake?

Without an answer to those questions, how did they manage to sell Howard Hughes on being an ally to *Stromboli*? Ingrid was close to hating Hughes. He was the opposite of her openness. She felt that he was after her for nothing but sex. And she had very little respect for the films he had made. But Cary Grant was the mutual friend who insisted that they meet, and then Hughes told Ingrid that he had bought RKO for her. He would pay for the picture. In all of this, Hughes virtually ignored Rossellini, though it was by now apparent that the two were joined by more than just a letter from out of nowhere. When told the idea of *Stromboli* Hughes was appalled or bewildered – why give up on the chance to dress Ingrid in beautiful clothes? He could see nothing of what might be new in the venture and he only wanted it in the way a tycoon might want a new curiosity. But the three parties made a deal whereby

RKO would put up most of the $1 million that *Stromboli* would take. By then that sum was moderate for an American picture but outlandish for an Italian film.

Ingrid set out for Rome in the spring of 1949 to make the picture. That's all it was, she claimed. But years later she would admit that she was in love with Rossellini, and that she believed he offered solutions to all the blocked situations in which she found herself. The Italian public treated the couple like a festival and Ingrid believed that the sun and the warmth were opening her up. She wrote to Petter, in America with Pia, to say she didn't think she could come back. She and Roberto took a ship from Sicily headed for Stromboli itself. And once on the island, it began: the world's press trying to prove a scandalous romance and struggling to work out its own equation of disapproval and need.

The weeks on that supposedly desolate island could make a movie. There was the considerable strain of the filming, especially when the volcano erupted. There was Ingrid's having to accustom herself to the ways and economics of neo-realism with few shared languages. There was the real love affair and the invasion of press people sent to prove it. And now began an avalanche of letters from friends and Hollywood people trying to explain the peril. Joe Steele felt it might all blow over after one film, if nothing was insisted on. There was a letter from Joseph Breen of the Motion Pictures Production Association, explaining that Ingrid risked destroying her career. There were letters from Petter and Pia and lawyers, and they were calling for a divorce. And Ingrid would not stop making statements that only showed how confused she was. At last, the agent, Lew Wasserman (who now represented her), called on one of his most trusted assistants to go to Stromboli and get her to shut up. That assistant was Kay Brown. Anything else? Yes, amid the island's epic and parable-like wildness a director and his actress conceived a child.

It wasn't just that Ingrid had had a child out of wedlock, though, it was that she had told Hedda Hopper she was not pregnant. Of course, that's another joke, or an attempt at it, but it's also a dire signal of how close censoriousness had come to that larger paranoia known as McCarthyism. In a way, the most splendid naivety Ingrid displayed in this whole event was the blithe ability to offend and alarm just about everyone. Somehow she managed to make the dilemma of Joan of Arc seem commonplace.

So, it's important to talk about *Stromboli* before we get to the comic frenzy of international outrage. I cannot suggest that *Stromboli* is a great film, a tidy film or any kind of conventional success. But it is an unforgettable failure, and an incident in film history worthy of both the hysterical moment and the comically ill-adjusted aspirations of Ingrid and Roberto. Some night they must have yielded to love-making if only to escape the insoluble contradictions in the rest of their lives. For here was Ingrid, so lately frustrated and infuriated by the meticulous fuss of one of the great directors of the

With Rossellini, making *Stromboli*

world, driven to dismay when actors on the rocky slopes of Stromboli had strings tied to their toes so that they would know when to utter at the jerk of the director's arm. Realism, neo-realism, naturalism were no easy answer or absolution when Roberto Rossellini was short of money, short of script, half out of his mind with his good luck, the rest of him demolished by the bad. And there was Ingrid, not so long ago a radiant nun for Leo McCarey, having to discover the spiritual ordeal of a Lithuanian woman as the volcano erupted.

A great deal is awkward and clumsy and beside the point (like the documentary on tuna fishing), but this strange rapture keeps coming back to shots of Ingrid and her island – and it is as if somehow someone had combined the eyes of Werner Herzog, Douglas Sirk and Robert Bresson! At the very end without any remaining doubt, you feel that this woman – actress as much as role – has been brought to exhausted confrontation with her question: what the fuck am I doing here? At the very end, the film comes together – we feel that the woman has seen the need for a god, even if she can't yet discern the figure itself. But you feel the wildness and the danger – rather as in the silent classic *The Wind* where Lillian Gish seems to have been reduced to a chaos more potent than anything her character understands. So there at last, you have the nexus of this very muddled time in Ingrid's life: in other words, how can the greatest actress in the world find fresh challenge in this cockamamie attempt at realism with this adorable madcap Rossellini without making an idiot of herself?

Well, you can't always have everything and as Petter
Lindstrom might have observed quietly to himself, for
years now, the American years, Ingrid Bergman had had
whatever she wanted.

The frenzy continued, as follows: in the evening of
2 February 1950, a son, Robertino, was born to Ingrid
and Roberto. This was a little less than two weeks before
their film was set to open in New York. In the months
before that opening, the Hughes organization had convinced itself they had a bestseller on their hands. They
therefore proposed to buy out the interests of star and
director: they offered $600,000, and Ingrid and Roberto
had refused it. But then at the last moment the reports
of the birth undid the whole enterprise. In Rome,
Ingrid received cables and letters not just from show-
business people (who had understood the tenor of her
private life), but from ordinary members of the public
in a tirade of abuse as innocent as the way fan letters
speak of love.

And it's not to be shrugged off as stupid and ungen-
erous. Ingrid Bergman had never been quite simply the
world's foremost 'natural actress', as David Selznick
intended, but the public bought her for her sincerity. It
was true that once or twice she had been a scarlet
woman on screen – in *Saratoga Trunk* and *Arch of Triumph*. But those films had not done well and the public
was led to regard her as an amalgam of all the great
roles she had had: Ilsa Lund, the spirit of noble refu-

gees; Maria, the virtuous peasant girl whose scars are removed by true love: Paula, the wife who overcomes her wicked husband; the honourable, saving shrink in *Spellbound*; the woman redeemed in *Notorious*. And let's not forget Sister Benedict and Joan of Lorraine. The public had believed in these stories, and they had responded by giving Ingrid their love and support. So it was natural of them to think that she supported them, or at least sustained their faith. This may not happen much any more with actors and actresses – and that is a large part of what has been lost in the magic of the movie experience. So it is easier for actors personally – but less so, too. If you want to realize how much less, look at what happened to Ingrid Bergman.

Edwin C. Johnson, Democratic Senator for Colorado, spoke in the Senate on 14 March 1950: 'Mr President, now that the stupid film about a pregnant woman and a volcano has exploited America with the usual finesse, to the mutual delight of RKO and the debased Rossellini, are we merely to yawn wearily, greatly relieved that this hideous thing is finished and then forget it? I hope not. A way must be found to protect the people in the future against that sort of gyp.'

The Senator proposed a bill that might license films according to the behaviour of their makers. Ingrid 'had perpetrated an assault upon the institution of marriage'. He called her 'a powerful influence for evil'. And then came the little bleat of the hurt child: for this woman had once been Senator Johnson's personal favourite

among movie stars. As for now, she was an alien, guilty
of moral turpitude, who should no longer be allowed to
set foot in America.

For a moment, the theatre-owners of America wondered if they would be put to a loyalty test. Then, like all
honest trimmers, they proposed a compromise: they'd
see how *Stromboli* did first and then only ban it if it was
a wicked success. Did some people stay away from
Bergman's films? Undoubtedly. Enough to determine
her career? Unlikely. Fortune came to the aid of prig-
gishness everywhere in that audiences proved to be dis-
mayed and perplexed by the films Ingrid made with
Rossellini. David Selznick gathered that Ingrid had
pretty much had enough after *Stromboli*. She had seen
the limits to the new ways of working and hungered for
a return to factory decadence.

But there were other issues: Ingrid sought a Mexican
divorce so that she could marry Rossellini as quickly as
possible. But in America, Petter won custody of Pia,
and the child herself (13 by then) gave some pretty devastating testimony against the mother. I suspect that the
furore could have been settled more quickly but for the
children and everyone's need to save face. Ingrid was in
a turmoil over Pia – in part because she realized how
much she had always neglected the girl. And now she
was an Italian Momma: in June 1952, she gave birth to
twin girls, Isotta and Isabella. All of a sudden, they were
a family of five.

*   *   *

And then, just as the knowing world had reason to point to Ingrid's folly, her reckless self-indulgence in going to Italy, she made a film that justified the entire adventure.

At the outset of *Europa '51*, Irene Girard (Ingrid Bergman) is driving a svelte limousine with her little dog sitting beside her. The unspoken comment on her life is a model for the film as a whole where matters are shown, not indicated. She is in a hurry. She is late. And the dog sits patiently beside her, staring at the road. Irene is late for a society dinner at her own residence – a luxurious apartment in the city. So she arrives in a hurry and tends to brush her little boy, Michel, aside. She has to check the table and the cooking. She has to bathe and change for the dinner. Her husband (Alexander Knox) understands this, so he doesn't presume upon her time. But Michel wants to see her, to be seen by her. He wants conversation. He gets a glance and a word and then the guests are arriving. It is one evening, but it is revealed to us with a masterly, critical distance. All of a sudden, someone is making this film.

During dinner, the boy has a fall. It is mysterious. There is a dangerous staircase in the apartment, but at the hospital – he has broken his hip – there is a suggestion that the boy fell deliberately. To win attention, or because he was in despair? Already, this question hangs in the air. The doctors say the boy will recover, but he dies – what do doctors ever know, compared with those who observe life?

Irene is on the cusp herself – is she guilty and bereft

at the loss of a son, or does she begin to perceive more profound cracks in the substance of life? One of her dinner guests that first night is a Communist, the publisher of a magazine of ideas. He assumes the task of educating her. He has her meet a poor family where a child may be lost because of lack of means. Irene is shown the harsh details of labour. She becomes a friend to the poor, and so gradually she is perceived as a traitor to her own class. She befriends a prostitute who dies. Her husband puts her in a mental institution. After all, she is living beyond the conventional code of charity that applies at her dinner parties. She wants to live the life of the suffering. At the end of the film she is committed to an asylum and she looks through the barred window at the helpless poverty she sees outside.

The most remarkable transition from *Stromboli* is the degree to which Rossellini has learned to look at Ingrid, and how to depict her in his kind of film. *Stromboli*, after all, was conceived before director and actress had met, and it is a flagrant confrontation of unknowns – with melodrama as the inevitable result. But whereas some people complained how in *Stromboli* the Lithuanian refugee was uninspiringly dressed, in *Europa '51* Ingrid has a wardrobe as befits a Roman socialite whose husband is the Italian representative of a major American corporation. Rossellini knows Ingrid now, knows that she is rich, much partied and well dressed. Her character is named 'Irene' and that could easily be a reference to Irene Selznick, one of Ingrid's confidantes and a woman who was famous for being a pretty hopeless mother. But the links are more intimate: Michel is very much a Pia-like child in Irene's sense of herself – the child Ingrid may have idealized and forgotten at the same time. So the documentary instincts in Rossellini, the taste for political realism, have focused on this actress who came to him from heaven. It is a picture about her, but colder than heaven.

Yet, if we translate *Europa '51* into a Hollywood picture of the 1950s – and there are such things, like the films of Douglas Sirk – then the most striking thing about this film is the absence of endearing or ingratiating close-ups, or the feeling that we are meant to love the star. The character dispels stardom, its glamour and its hallowed self-pity. Instead, Rossellini has found a way of photographing Ingrid – it is absolutely new in her career – so that we are put in the position of jurors instead of lovers. We may feel for her, or on her behalf, but we are cut off from identification. We see her as a force moving in her own field, a woman condemned by her own selfishness to an hysterical effort to rediscover her soul. Did Ingrid Bergman understand this or the extent to which Rossellini had seen through her? Nothing in what she said about working with him suggests that she did. This was a more conventional picture, but it was a great failure, too. Yet everything we know about Ingrid had been employed in what amounts to a critique of her – not cruel or brutal, but completely free from sentimentality, too. She is a test case, a figure in a parable or a sociological treatise – that is how close this film comes to being a documentary of Ingrid Bergman herself. She can participate in the full political life of her times only as an actress.

There are moments in *Europa '51* when Irene observes the cityscape – it is not grand, but it is alienating – and we are on the edge of that passage in *La Notte*, say, where Michelangelo Antonioni lets Jeanne Moreau wander in the outskirts of Milan, observing the desultory mosaic of life. It is a kind of modernism that would affect Jean-Luc Godard, too, and it is an eloquent extension of political cinema in which a character (or an actress or a star) is quietly drowned in the ocean of unhealed, unmediated reality. I'm far from sure that Ingrid Bergman felt or saw that aspect of *Europa '51*. I think she believed she was playing a kind of Dostoyevskyan saint, a woman who turns on her own wealth by taking on the unhealed wounds in society. Ingrid is still lovely – well dressed, her hair coiffed, her close-ups often loaded with feeling – but her beauty is nothing but the imprint of loneliness. If a true search is a way of admitting loss or failure, then it's right to say that Ingrid Bergman was never again the romantic actress she had been, the one who thought Courage was enough.

Europa '51 was a disaster in Europe and in America (though it had critical admirers, especially in France). There was now very little hope left that their bold creative partnership was going to satisfy either of them.

Rossellini had wanted to make money. Ingrid had had a vague dream of art or something more conclusive. Instead, they had gathered a mass of scandal and the hostility that went with it, three young children for a woman who was seldom a natural mother, and diminishing funds. To make matters worse, Ingrid had realized that another of Roberto's natural talents – as a womanizer – was unstoppable. He was having affairs, largely because he felt they were expected of him. In the increasingly difficult years that followed they were both of them looking for a way out.

There were other invitations. In Italy alone, offers came from Luchino Visconti, Vittorio de Sica, Federico Fellini and Franco Zeffirelli for Ingrid to work with them. But Rossellini was jealous of any rival, especially if they could find a good vehicle for Ingrid. So he turned down every offer without allowing her the freedom to make up her own mind. Increasingly, Ingrid began to see that there had been a bond between Roberto and Anna Magnani that couldn't be replaced:

Maybe that was because they were the same stock, a good mix. We weren't a good mix. The world hated the Rossellini version of me, so nothing worked. And he was stuck with me. What did he want with an international star? Nothing. He didn't know what to write for me. And, of course, by this time we both knew it. It was something we did not talk about. But the silences between us grew longer – the silences when I didn't dare to say anything because I would hurt his feelings. Roberto would take whatever I said, and, unhappy as he was, would make a scene about it. He liked to fight. And besides the traumas of our artistic life, our increasing debts worried me enormously.

They clutched at Joan of Arc again, though this time the project was a staged oratorio, written by Paul Claudel, with music by Arthur Honegger. In a version produced and directed by Rossellini, they opened at the Teatro San Carlo in Naples in 1953, and then went on tour. Later in the same year a film was made of the production – though rather more to keep a record than to reconceive it in movie terms. *Siamo Donne* was the kind of film much enjoyed in Italy in the '50s – it was a film of episodes, short stories designed to feature the actresses Isa Miranda, Anna Magnani (directed by Luchino Visconti), Alida Valli and Bergman (directed by Rossellini), It was a very minor affair in which Ingrid played a woman who had a feud with a neighbour over a hen.

Againt all odds Ingrid and Roberto rallied with their next film, and again I have to suggest that the intelligence and the emotional life of the picture come from Rossellini rather than from Bergman. *Viaggio in Italia* is generally known as *Journey to Italy* in the English-speaking world. It concerns an English couple, Alex and Katherine Joyce. They have been married a long time, too long, and the pretext of their visit to Italy is to complete the sale of a house they have owned together. The house stands for a lost happiness just as the journey is a step towards divorce. It was obvious that Ingrid would play Katherine, but Rossellini agreed – if he would consent – to the casting of George Sanders as the husband.

Of course, Sanders and Ingrid had worked together once before – in *Rage in Heaven* – but they were not friends. On the other hand, Sanders had won the supporting actor Oscar in 1950 in *All About Eve*, and he seems to have felt some dismay that he was so often typecast and so seldom asked to deliver a real acting job. Sanders was uncertain why he had been cast. He was a depressive (despite his colourful lifestyle – he was married to Zsa Zsa Gabor), but still he made every conscientious effort to believe that Rossellini was a great director. In fact, Sanders the actor was raised in the Hollywood tradition, and he expected a script, reliable lines to learn, and emphatic scenes to play. Just a few weeks in Italy was enough to put him on the brink of a nervous breakdown.

Sanders loathed the uncertainties in Rossellini's shooting method, and his grimness shows. So once again Rossellini had pierced the glamorous armour of stars to get at the naked discomfort of the actors. They are ill-suited; they are stiltedly polite; they seem exactly like a couple that deserves merciful separation. But then Rossellini rebuilds. Small, inadvertent signs of sympathy surface, and in the end – at a religious demonstration on the city streets – they are reunited by shared fear and dismay. Will this save the marriage? It seems unlikely.

But Rossellini manages to end his film on a point of enigma. Something about life in Italy has reawakened the sour, dormant spirits of this husband and wife. It is almost as if, on the point of his own divorce, Rossellini the artist has found a way to say, and to ask himself as much as his wife, 'And yet . . . ?'

Viaggio in Italia is not as cogent as *Europa '51*, but it is more moving. It is the logical destination of Irene Girard to be imprisoned: that is where her self-conscious martyrdom is headed. But the Joyces are more ordinary (even if the name was meant to refer to James Joyce). They are Northern souls caught in the Italian light – and this may have been one of the chief lessons that Rossellini drew from his liaison with Ingrid. They are cynical, bored, exhausted. But such things as the ruins of Pompeii, and the sheer experience of Italy – the warmth, the light, the human untidiness – test their imprisoning self-regard. Shot in deep focus and long takes, *Viaggio in Italia* is like a novel or a ruminative travel essay, and the influence on Antonioni is unmistakable. As if for the first time in her life, Ingrid Bergman is simply the available actress, the figure in a landscape – she is never close to being a heroine, a reliable quantity or a guiding light. At this nearly last step, it is as if Rossellini has seen through all the mythology that Ingrid Bergman was 'magic'. She is mundane – but he has found a way of liking her, or thinking well of her after their separation.

* * *

In which case, sentimentalists might wish they had accepted *Viaggio* as their farewell, and had not made the film that is variously called *La Paura*, or *Fear*. It is not without quality – indeed, as a perverse remake of *Gaslight*, it can be very intriguing – but still, it has a dank air to it, like a room filled with the cancer and contempt of a failed marital reconciliation. It is deeply upsetting, a film noir, in which the shadow feels like the blood of the characters. The sound is very strained, as in all of Ingrid's Rossellini fims, and Bergman can seem very stilted with awkward English dialogue. But it's worse than that: we feel she is being strangled – that there is no longer enough air available. She reported herself that the German actor playing with her in *Fear*, Mathias Wieman, said to her one day, 'It's impossible. You can't go on working with him. You'll go insane.' Ingrid said she was startled by the remark – but that is the actress taking refuge in 'surprise'. You can see death in the film getting ready. In grim coincidence, as *Fear* was being made the news came from IndoChina that Robert Capa had been killed. The photographer had been looking for a better angle for a picture and stepped on a landmine.

Fear comes from a novel by Stefan Zweig. It is set in Germany, and was actually filmed in English- and German-speaking versions simultaneously (with Bergman speaking her own German). The married couple, the Wagners, run an experimental chemical laboratory where they are trying to find new drugs to prevent pain.

They conduct experiments with live animals – rats. The
man (Wieman) is the experimenter, while the company
is run by his wife, Irene (Bergman).

But as the story starts, Irene is involved in an affair
with a musician. She is torn about it. She feels fear, but
she cannot stop the affair. Then a young woman, Miss
Schultze (Renate Manhardt), comes to her. She too was
in love with the musician, but he dropped her for Irene.
And now, in revenge, this woman – attractive yet odi-
ous – starts to blackmail Irene. Unless she is given
money, she will tell the husband.

When I spoke of a perverse version of *Gaslight*, I
meant that whereas in the Hamilton adaptation Paula is
an innocent woman driven to the point of insanity, now
in *Fear* Irene is guilty, and she is pushed to the brink of
suicide – something she would manage by injecting herself with a poison given to the rats. By then, however,
she has learned that the entire blackmail scheme, and
the mounting ordeal she faces (there is a ring Miss
Schultze has stolen, a ring that has to be reclaimed) are
all the work of her husband, who seems ready to treat
her like one of his own rats hanging in the balance.

It is a hideous intrigue, and Bergman is good enough to
make the scenes of mania credible and heart-wrenching.
But the ending is dreadful, many scenes are mishandled,
and the overall conceit – that lying is like acting – is not
made clear. But the claustrophobia in the plot, the savage lighting, the hints of allusions to German history
and the great gloom in Wieman's husband are not easily

forgotten. It is hard to think of a divorce judge who would not give an order of separation on the strength of the movie.

One person who could read the tea leaves was Kay Brown. Yes, she was still an agent and still a part of Ingrid's life. (I knew Kay Brown a little, late in her life, and it is hard to think of any 'unknown' person who gave more to show business in her lifetime.) She foresaw the chance of Ingrid making an American comeback, and she had prompted Twentieth Century-Fox into buying the movie rights to a play by Marcelle Maurette about a refugee who has lost her memory who is hired to impersonate the surviving child of the last Tzar – but who may be the real child.

When Brown and the director Anatole Litvak both suggested Ingrid Bergman for the role, Fox objected. They said that Bergman was box-office death. There would be riots and demonstrations. They, and David O. Selznick, preferred the idea of Jennifer Jones. But Ingrid would be a heck of a coup, said Kay Brown, coming back from the dead to regain her aristocratic rights. Litvak had asked Ingrid to do *The Snake Pit* earlier and she had said Roberto wouldn't allow it. So Olivia de Havilland had done it and won an Oscar nomination. Litvak insisted. Kay Brown argued. And at last Ingrid was offered the part – along with $200,000. (I told you, Kay Brown was the real thing.)

To avoid any incidents, it was decided to make the

film in England. When Ingrid told Roberto he repeated
the warning he had made often before – that he would
kill himself – she called his bluff. He went off to India
to make a documentary that would determine the later
direction of his career, and find him a third wife. At
the same time, Ingrid agreed to play the lead in *Tea and
Sympathy* on the French stage.

With Helen Hayes and Yul Brynner as her supports,
Ingrid went back to conventional film-making on *Anastasia*. The imagination of screenwriter Arthur Laurents
gave her the hokey money scene in which the pretender
comes before the grandmother figure, the Grand Duchess (Hayes). (As she enters this crucial audience, her
chief backer or director – Brynner – whispers, 'Courage!') No, says the Duchess, this is not Anastasia. Then
Ingrid coughs. What's the matter, asks the Duchess,
have you a cold? No it's just that I cough when I am
nervous – it's an old habit. And the Grand Duchess
cracks because the only person she ever knew with that
habit was the infant Anastasia. Is this a great show – or
do you want to call it history? The hills are alive with the
sound of coughing.

Anastasia is a pretty bad movie, worse than the things
Ingrid had done in Hollywood ten years earlier. But it
makes a feeble gesture towards being a study in acting.
After all, this woman picked off the streets is hired to
impersonate Anastasia, and then she begins to wonder
if she might not be the real thing. Anatole Litvak is not
available for these ironies – think how Rossellini might

Anastasia?

have treated them. But the whole thing allows for some piercing comments on acting. Akim Tamiroff (playing one of the con men) says something about Stanislavsky urging that acting is believing you are the part until the belief is so great that the actor has to be fired. Tamiroff, of course, had himself been trained at the Moscow Art Theatre. On second thoughts, this subject needs not Rossellini, but Preston Sturges.

Anastasia opened in December 1956, and America was charmed by it. In truth, Ingrid was 41 (and ready to pass for older), but the public spirit of sentimental forgiveness was so great they never noticed the age disparity: set in 1928, the film's Anastasia should be 27. Against that the picture had over $4 million in rentals, resuming Ingrid's very high average in that field. The New York Film Critics voted to give her the best actress prize and her first return to American soil was to receive it. There were no unpleasant demonstrations on the street, but large, fond crowds came out to welcome her. Nothing in her life had ever inspired unkindness.

She was on stage in Paris doing *Tea and Sympathy* (to great acclaim) by the time the Academy caught up. Though the film's only other nomination was for music, *Anastasia* secured a best actress nomination for Ingrid. Her rivals were Carroll Baker in *Baby Doll*, Katharine Hepburn in *The Rainmaker*, Nancy Kelly in *The Bad Seed* and Deborah Kerr in *The King and I*. (Incidentally, that meant that Elizabeth Taylor was not nominated for *Giant*, nor Marilyn Monroe for *Bus Stop*, nor Ava Gardner for *Bhowani Junction*. Nor even Julie Harris in *East of Eden*.) On the night itself, Cary Grant stepped up to accept the statuette in Ingrid's absence and he sent a message to her over the airwaves to do all he could to welcome her back.

The divorce from Rossellini was finalized in 1957. A year later, she married Lars Schmidt, a Swedish theatre producer, a man she met very soon after the Oscar, in Paris, where he tried to get her to play the lead on stage in Tennessee Williams' *Cat on a Hot Tin Roof*. There was a reunion with Pia (19 in 1957), though Petter Lindstrom was remarried by then.

In a way, that's the end of the story. After *Anastasia*, Ingrid would make another thirteen films, plus several films for television. She would win a supporting actress Oscar in the Agatha Christie adaptation, playing a tall mouse in *Murder on the Orient Express*, in 1974, and she won an Emmy for her performance as Golda Meir in *A Woman Called Golda*. She made pictures for Jean Renoir (*Elena et les Hommes*) and for Ingmar Bergman (*Autumn Sonata*). She had a big hit with Cary Grant in *Indiscreet*. She won tears as Gladys Aylward, leading young children out of Red China, in *The Inn of the Sixth Happiness*. She appeared with her daughter Isabella and with Charles Boyer again in Vincente Minnelli's *A Matter of Time*. She danced with Goldie Hawn in *Cactus Flower*. And she did several classic plays on stage over the years, though her fellow-actors learned that she often missed lines and cues. When asked once how she had got through all the turmoil and the trouble she said, 'A bad memory'. It was a great Ingrid Bergman line, something Ilsa Lund could have said with a flourish, but which can signal real loss in your sixties.

But the sum of those years, 1957 to 1982, when she died on her 67th birthday, would not qualify her for this series of books. In that last era, she is a conventional, middle-aged actress with several deeply felt performances, but she is no longer a movie star, a unique icon, a message made out of cinematography, or a person who could destroy the dreams of millions if she made a 'mistake' in life. How could she be? How could anyone live at that fever-pitch for more than a few years? As it was, Ingrid Bergman was only really Ingrid from *Casablanca* to *Under Capricorn* – seven years.

I'm not sure that many have lasted longer – though Bette Davis did, and Katharine Hepburn and even Elizabeth Taylor. Still, the end of the stardom I am talking about is exhausting and self-destructive – it takes away the subject's youth and need as well as their looks, and it threatens a kind of boredom or disappointment in the public that can be as cruel as it is casual. Of course, seven years when you are young can pass in a blink, so that you hardly appreciate it before it is over. If Ingrid felt the first hint of boredom in the late '40s when she wrote the letter to Rossellini, then she certainly learned to regret the consequence of impulsive actions. But it's just as possible that the burden on her of carrying the ignorant love of so many strangers was bound to make her impulsive and drawn to folly. To think that you are known by strangers can be maddening.

Not that the Rossellini years deserve to be written off as a misguided excursion. I have taken pains in this book to describe those films properly, and in a way that might make you want to see them fifty and more years later. The adventure or the journey was natural and important, for there were at least two types of film and two ways of thinking about cinema available in 1949. It might be the grand old Hollywood scheme, or it might be something new – smaller, more local, cheaper, less dreamlike, more disturbing, more difficult or artistic. That choice still exists. For 'Hollywood' has never quite acknowledged its own death – it enjoys the high jinks of the Ghost's role too much. And so, the red carpet of the Academy rolls out every year to symbolize an empire with amazing limitations (and absurd power).

Roberto Rossellini is an important director in the history of film, a very intelligent man with his art, even if he was a stereotype rogue as a man and a husband. There is a good deal of smothered comedy in the meeting of Ingrid and Roberto, and it is true that not one of their films came anywhere near reaching the sort of audience that swallowed *The Bells of St Mary's, For Whom the Bell Tolls* or *Spellbound*. But the Rossellini films are extraordinary, and *Europa '51* and *Viaggio in Italia*, are of a very high quality, even if they show an Ingrid Bergman being reduced from stardom, beauty and limitless loveability to a real, awkward woman. That deal was always on the cards, just as Rossellini had to learn that Ingrid was not going to make him rich and famous. Infamous was second best, and extended penury – or money-worries – is the most lasting model there will ever be for serious film-makers. And if you want to prove the consistency and the sinister rhyme-scheme in the two parts of Ingrid's career, just show a double-bill of *Gaslight* and *Fear*. Yes, *Gaslight* is more fun, better made and more entertaining, and I do not have any wish to belittle entertainment. But *Gaslight* settles for being fun, and *Fear* reaches out – beyond its grasp, to be sure – for something that will not go away. So film or movie should be a medium that gives us both? Well, we have both, and Ingrid Bergman's is one of the few careers that makes that so clear.

The one film that needs to be examined closely is *Autumn Sonata*. Ingrid and Ingmar Bergman had known each other since the mid 1960s, having been introduced by Lars Schmidt. They had talked sometimes about the desirability of working together. Ingmar had written her a letter promising such a thing. Then, as she prepared to head the jury at Cannes in 1972, Ingrid found the old letter that had that promise, added a fresh question to it, and dropped it in Ingmar's pocket when they met at Cannes. A reply came along and then, a little later, a real project: did Ingrid feel she could act the part of Liv Ullmann's mother? By 1978, Ingrid was 63 and

Ullmann 39 – so the numbers did fit. Ullmann met Ingrid and was delighted at how straightforward she was. What Ingmar wanted was a small film – about a mother and daughter – to be filmed in the Swedish language but in Norway. The parties agreed to that. And Ingmar wrote a script. The first version seemed to Ingrid like the script for a six-hour film – it was so thorough, so novelistic, so searching, but she said she thought it was promising.

This is the story of *Autumn Sonata*: Charlotte (Ingrid) is a world-famous concert pianist. For years, she had a lover and a musical associate – named Leonardo – but he has just died. On hearing that, Eva (Ullmann), Charlotte's daughter, writes to her mother, inviting her to come and stay in the rural Norwegian village where her husband, Viktor, is the pastor. Charlotte arrives and she realizes that Eva's house is also the home of Helena, Eva's mentally handicapped sister. Years earlier, Charlotte had put Helena in a home, but then Charlotte quietly chose to have her sister released and to do all she could to look after her.

Soon after Charlotte's arrival, Eva plays a Chopin prelude for her. In fact, Charlotte is impressed by the feeling in her daughter's performance, but then she elects to demonstrate her own superiority by playing it again herself – with brilliance, of course, but with less feeling perhaps. In the middle of the night that follows, mother and daughter find themselves awake and Eva launches into a scathing attack to the effect that her

mother never felt anything in truth, but did everything
for her professional career. Charlotte is shattered, and
she asks for just a sign of love, a touch. She admits that
she was always afraid of her own daughter. The next
day, the mother goes away and the daughter tries to
write a letter of apology.

The cast assembled for a reading of the script and
the director noted that 'Ingrid . . . read her part in a
sonorous voice with gestures and expressions . . . So
many false intonations had not been heard since the
1930s.' Ingrid told him the script was dull; she said
repeating the Chopin prelude would be painful. There
were quarrels and then there was news from London
(test results) that Ingrid's cancer might be returning.
She began to work hard and she gave the production
some old strips of film of herself as a child – films
taken by her father.

Was there a sense of rivalry between the two Bergmans? They fought, and then laughed about it, but it
was never an easy relationship. A documentary was
made on the filming, one that showed Ingrid as tough,
brave, difficult and heartfelt. Afterwards, she watched
the documentary and said, 'I should have seen this
before I started filming.'

Then, one afternoon, she and her director were sitting together, waiting for the lights to be placed. Ingmar
would write later, 'It was semi-dusk and we were each in
a corner of a shabby old leather sofa. Ingrid made a
gesture very rare for an actress – she ran her hand over

In *Autumn Sonata*, with Liv Ullman

her face, several times. Then she drew a deep breath and looked at me, without friendliness or trying to make contact. "You know I'm living on borrowed time."'

Autumn Sonata is a gruelling experience, no matter the Bergman touch or the skill of the two lead actresses. That is not uncommon with Ingmar Bergman, a man whose misanthropic streak seldom needed watering. I think anyone with a knowledge of Ingrid's life can see a rather gratuitous exploitation here. Ingrid herself seems not to have complained about the assault – however justified – on a mother who abandons a daughter to pursue her art. But the 'Leonardo' figure is a daub from history rather than a useful construct. Over the decades Ingmar Bergman himself had been obsessed with the question of how far an artist must ignore his own life – and Ingmar Bergman had a heavier list of collateral casualties than Ingrid. Ingmar never quite had her charm, and there's no way that the best photography of Ingrid at 60 (by Sven Nykvist) can recapture it. Youth and the camera know no substitutes.

Of course, we don't have to ask what happened to Ilsa Lund. She goes on forever, and that curious privilege is true of every achievement in stardom. In general, actresses have a more vibrant but much shorter peak. It is still 'natural' on screen for Cooper to have Grace Kelly in *High Noon*, or for Bogart to woo Lauren Bacall in the smoochy smoky rooms they kept at Warner Brothers. The smoke killed Bogart, and Lauren Bacall would become a harsh mockery of Slim. It hardly matters. The youthful moment and the close-up that asks what are they thinking – they go on forever. That Ingrid Bergman still needs to hear 'As Time Goes By' again – it is her only way of stopping time. And the need still matters.

A Note on Sources

The central work is *Ingrid Bergman: My Story*, by Ingrid herself and Alan Burgess (New York, 1980). It consists of an 'objective' narrative and passages from Ingrid herself. It is useful and fascinating, not least in teaching us that Ingrid did not always tell the truth. Then the reader should go to Laurence Leamer's *As Time Goes By: The Life of Ingrid Bergman* (New York, 1986).

Other books of value include Joseph Henry Steele, *Ingrid Bergman: An Intimate Portrait* (New York, 1959); Don Ranvaud, *Roberto Rossellini* (London, 1981); Irene Selznick, *A Private View* (New York, 1983). Ingrid Bergman's papers are at Wesleyan University.

Filmography

1946   *American Creed*
        Notorious
1948   *Arch of Triumph*
        Joan of Arc (Oscar nomination for Best Actress in
                a Leading Role)
1949   *Under Capricorn*
1950   *Stromboli*
1952   *The Greatest Love*
1954   *Journey to Italy*
        Fear
        Joan of Arc at the Stake
1956   *Elena and Her Men*
        Anastasia (Oscar win for Best Actress in a Leading
                Role)
1958   *Indiscreet*
        The Inn of the Sixth Happiness
1961   *Goodbye Again*
        Kolka, My Friend
1964   *The Visit*
        The Yellow Rolls-Royce
1967   *Stimulantia*
1969   *Cactus Flower*
1970   *A Walk in the Spring Rain*
1973   *From the Mixed-Up Files of Mrs. Basil E. Frankweiler*
1974   *Murder on the Orient Express* (Oscar win for Best
                Actress in a Supporting Role)
1976   *A Matter of Time*
1978   *Autumn Sonata* (Oscar nomination for Best Actress
                in a Leading Role)

Picture Credits